1969

W9-ABR-671

book may be kept

JONATHAN SWIFT

ROMANTIC AND CYNIC MORALIST

JONATHAN SWIFT

ROMANTIC AND CYNIC MORALIST

Jack G. Gilbert

UNIVERSITY OF TEXAS PRESS, AUSTIN & LONDON

Library of Congress Catalog Card No. 66–15709
Copyright © 1966 by Jack G. Gilbert
All Rights Reserved

Printed in the United States of America
by the Printing Division of The University of Texas, Austin
Bound by Universal Bookbindery, Inc., San Antonio

For Martha,
Jacquelyn, and Geoffrey

ACKNOWLEDGMENTS

A sober study of Swift's thought should begin with an apology for treating a playful, witty subject in a plain, serious manner. This is necessary in order to exorcise the spirits of Grub Street, who have taken consummate revenge on their enemy, Jonathan Swift. Although this study stresses the serious value of Swift's writings, it is written in a spirit of gratitude for the refreshing and cheering qualities of Swift's humor.

I owe an especial debt of gratitude to Professor Ernest Campbell Mossner, of The University of Texas, for advice and assistance in the preparation of this study.

My thanks are also due to Professors A. P. Brogan, Oscar Maurer, and Gordon Mills (of The University of Texas); to Professor Mary Wagoner and Dean George Branam (of Louisiana State University in New Orleans); and to Professor John V. Price (of the University of Edinburgh).

I am grateful to the staffs of two excellent libraries, The University of Texas Library and Huntington Library, for assistance in the conduct of the research.

A Louisiana State University Research Council grant enabled me to finish the research and to put the manuscript into final shape.

I am grateful to my wife and to Mrs. Mae Mackey for typing the final draft.

PERMISSIONS

Permission to quote from the following publications is gratefully acknowledged:

Hazlitt, William. *The Complete Works of William Hazlitt,* edited by P. P. Howe. London: J. M. Dent & Sons, Ltd., 1930.

Hobbes, Thomas. *Leviathan,* edited by Michael Oakeshott. Oxford: Basil Blackwell, 1960.

Johnson, Samuel. *Anecdotes of Samuel Johnson,* edited by S. C. Roberts. Cambridge: Cambridge University Press, 1932.

———. *Lives of the English Poets.* London: J. N. Dent, 1958 (Everyman's Library).

Lovejoy, Arthur O. *The Great Chain of Being.* Cambridge, Mass.:
Harvard University Press, 1964.

Machiavelli. *The Prince and the Discourses,* edited by Max Lerner.
New York: Random House, Inc., 1950.

Swift, Jonathan. *The Correspondence of Jonathan Swift,* edited by
F. F. Ball. London: George Bell & Sons, Ltd., 1910–1914.

————. *Journal to Stella,* edited by Harold Williams. Oxford: Clarendon Press, 1948.

————. *The Letters of Jonathan Swift to Charles Ford,* edited by D.
Nichol Smith. Oxford: Clarendon Press, 1935.

————. *The Poems of Jonathan Swift,* edited by Harold Williams.
Oxford: Clarendon Press, 1958.

————. *The Prose Works of Jonathan Swift,* edited by Herbert Davis.
Oxford: Basil Blackwell, 1939–1962.

METHOD OF CITATION

In quoting from books written before the twentieth century, I have preserved the original spelling and capitalization. I have made no attempt to reproduce italics and small capitals, and such tricks as italics within italics. In every case, however, I indicate when I have added italics.

I give references to *Gulliver's Travels* by citing part, chapter, and paragraph—since all readers may not use the text in Davis' edition of the *Prose Works*, XI, from which I quote. When it is necessary to refer to pages outside the four parts (the four voyages), I cite Davis' Volume XI by page; the reader should note, however, that pagination varies in the 1941 edition and the 1959 reprint, from which I quote.

ABBREVIATIONS

1. Within the text:

C...............*The Correspondence of Jonathan Swift*, ed. F. F. Ball. 6 vols. London: George Bell, 1910–1914.

J...............*Journal to Stella*, ed. Harold Williams. 2 vols. Oxford: Clarendon, 1948.

LF...............*The Letters of Jonathan Swift to Charles Ford*, ed. D. Nichol Smith. Oxford: Clarendon, 1935.

P...............*The Poems of Jonathan Swift*, ed. Harold Williams. 3 vols. Oxford: Clarendon, 1958.

PW...............*The Prose Works of Jonathan Swift*, ed. Herbert Davis. 13 vols. Oxford: Basil Blackwell, 1939–1962.

TS...............*The Prose Works of Jonathan Swift*, ed. Temple Scott. 12 vols. London: George Bell, 1897–1908.

2. In the notes:

Delany...............Patrick Delany. *Observations upon Lord Orrery's Remarks on the Life and Writings of Dr. Jonathan Swift*. London: W. Reeve, 1754.

Hawkesworth......"An Account of the Life of the Reverend Jonathan Swift," *The Works of Dr. Jonathan Swift*, I, ed. John Hawkesworth. London, 1766.

Johnson's *Life*....Samuel Johnson, "Jonathan Swift," *Lives of the English Poets,* II. London: J. M. Dent, 1958. (Everyman's Library).

Leviathan..........Thomas Hobbes, *Leviathan,* ed. Michael Oakeshott. Oxford: Basil Blackwell, 1960. I give chapter citations, with page references within parentheses.

Orrery.................John, Earl of Orrery. *Remarks on the Life and Writings of Dr. Jonathan Swift.* London: A. Millar, 1752.

Sheridan............Thomas Sheridan. *The Life of Rev. Jonathan Swift,* 2nd. ed. London: J. F. and C. Rivington, 1787.

Deane Swift.......*An Essay upon the Life, Writings, and Character of Dr. Jonathan Swift.* London: Charles Bathurst, 1755.

Scott..................."Memoirs of Jonthan Swift," *The Works of Swift,* I, ed. Sir Walter Scott, 2nd. ed. London: Bickers & Sons, 1883.

CONTENTS

JONATHAN SWIFT
Romantic and Cynic Moralist

PART I

Swift's Ethics

CHAPTER 1

Introduction

A full-scale biography of Swift's mind would be remarkable for what is omitted. Of the five conventional divisions of philosophy (metaphysics, logic, epistemology, ethics, and aesthetics), Swift evinced an interest in only the last two—the more practical, more human of the five. Although interested in a few aesthetic questions (mainly related to literature), Swift devoted his life and most of his work to problems which are ethical in the broadest sense (moral, social, political); his understanding of the function of a preacher was to "talk moralls" (LF, 2).

In other words, Swift was a humanist—to whom everything not immediately and usefully human is alien. His writings show no interest in scientific investigations of the day—except to condemn or wonder at irrationalities and absurdities. His comments on Berkeley, in his letters, show little awareness of Berkeley's critique of materialism. His library represents well his predilections: moral philosophy, belles-lettres, history.[1]

This salient abridgment of knowledge Swiftians have always recognized. Yet, while agreeing that Swift was above all a moralist, scholars have been less in agreement as to what kind of moralist he was. For example, Ricardo Quintana puts Swift in the Stoic school;[2] whereas Kathleen Williams depicts him as a virulent anti-Stoic Christian.[3] Curiously, as our knowledge of the intellectual history of the eighteenth century grows clearer (thanks to the efforts of men like A. O. Lovejoy, R. S. Crane, and Leo Strauss), our understanding of Swift obfuscates.

At the center of the quarrel about the school of moral philosophy to which Swift belongs is his most famous work, *Gulliver's Travels*. Those who agree with Swift's moral views, and those who disagree, invariably

[1] See Harold Williams, *Dean Swift's Library* (Cambridge: The University Press, 1932), pp. 38 ff.
[2] Ricardo Quintana, *The Mind and Art of Jonathan Swift* (London: Oxford University Press, 1953), pp. 59 ff.
[3] Kathleen Williams, *Jonathan Swift and the Age of Compromise* (Lawrence: University of Kansas Press, 1958), pp. 206 ff.

center their attention on *Gulliver,* which is (I believe) a repository of what Swift regarded as ethical wisdom. Although most studies of Swift make a similar assumption, the question, again, concerns the kind of ethical wisdom which *Gulliver* is supposed to contain: is it utopian or antiutopian, Stoic or anti-Stoic? Recent criticism has been marked by the tendency to seize upon a phrase or sentence from Swift's nonsatiric writings (e.g., the letters) and to use that phrase or sentence to elucidate the "meaning" of *Gulliver's Travels.*[4] This tendency suggests that a detailed study of Swift's concrete ethical judgments and statements ought to precede an analysis of *Gulliver's Travels*—or ought to be a desideratum in view of the selectivity of most critical studies.

It seemed to me thus reasonable to first outline the general directions of the complex body of Swift's ethical opinions and to then examine the ethical patterns of the satire in *Gulliver's Travels.* For purely formal reasons, I have dealt in turn with Swift's attacks on human failings (or vices, Chapter 2); Swift's praise of human excellences (or virtues, Chapter 3); and Swift's devotion to a heroic or romantic ideal (Chapter 4). If my purpose were only to stress the positive side of Swift's ethics Chapter 2 could easily be omitted—as could Chapter 5, which forms a counterpoint to Chapter 4 in elaborating on Swift's pessimistic social and religious doctrines. But such omission would distort the phenomena; Swift's thought varied over a lifetime, from occasion to occasion. I have tried to map out the main lines of this thought, faithfully representing the contradictory and ambiguous tendencies, in Chapters 2 through 5, which make up, consequently, something of a dialectic. It is possible, certainly, to simplify Swift into one or another system of belief; but the constructs of the historian of ideas do not, unfortunately, always correctly describe the complicated state of one man's mind.

This is not to suggest that the movement of ideas is irrelevant to a study of Swift's mind. Against the background of the struggle of ideas one can best discern the main tides and eddies of Swift's opinions.

It is a well-known paradox that what is called the Age of Reason is in fact the age in which reason died, or was killed. Our twentieth-century inclination to put "reason" in inverted commas is but a coroner's confirmation of demise. The classical doctrine, or rationalism (usually linked with the term "faculty psychology"), saw two divisions in man, emotion and reason—with elaborate subdivisions. Reason, of course, was the superior *de jure* if not *de facto.* As Hershel Baker observes:

    [4] This is true of most of the articles cited by R. S. Crane, "The Houyhnhnms, the Yahoos, and the History of Ideas," *Reason and the Imagination,* ed. J. A. Mazzeo (New York: Columbia University Press, 1962), pp. 231–232 n.

A Platonist, an Aristotelian, a Christian humanist would all agree that man's rational soul was his crown and his beatitude, and as such that it should enjoy what Spenser called its "dew regalitie." Through his reason, the faculty of his highest level of soul, man may attain genuine knowledge, or live a life of temperance and rational well-being, or become like the God whose divine attribute of reason he alone among animals shares.[5]

The major philosophers of the Age of Reason (Hobbes, Locke, Hume) opposed the old rationalism, especially its notion of "innate ideas." More than vestiges of this rationalism survived, however, in the writings of the Deists, of men like the Third Earl of Shaftesbury, of the Scottish common-sense school of philosophy, and of an occasional rationalist like Richard Price—and in the minds of those not-too-accurate reasoners, gentlemen. Enough of the old view survived in the mid-eighteenth century to give meaning to Hume's deft incongruity in the famous pronouncement that "Reason is, and ought only to be, the slave of the passions." More and more, in the hundred years 1650 to 1750, philosophers were insisting that man was essentially emotional.

The view of the antirationalistic empiricists that man acquired no ideas except through sense impressions facilitated, or congratulated, the work of experimental scientists, but created a problem for moral philosophers: all ideas coming from the senses, how do we develop ideas of good and evil? Two answers were given, historically. First, writers after Locke reinterpreted moral "ideas" as feelings or instincts. Innate ideas were thus preserved as innate emotions—for example, in the writings of the Moral Sense or Benevolist school (Shaftesbury, Hutcheson, Hume, Adam Smith).[6] Second, many philosophers, such as Hobbes and Locke, defined the good as pleasure (or the avoidance of pain), and thus tried to keep an experiential base for moral ideas. This egoistic hedonism (as in Locke's philosophy)[7] assumes that human beings act on the basis of securing their own pleasure, avoiding their own pain.

The old rationalistic moral doctine, conversely, had held that man could know (intuit) basic moral truths, that man could by natural reason know what was right and could pursue it, if he chose, regardless of the pleasure or pain involved. The difference of opinion—between the old and new views—ranges from the egoistic hedonism of utilitarians like Locke to the rationalistic concepts of human nobility held by those

[5] Herschel Baker, *The Dignity of Man: Studies in the Persistence of an Idea* (Cambridge: Harvard University Press, 1947), p. 288.

[6] See D. Daiches Raphael, *The Moral Sense* (London: Oxford University Press, 1947), especially pp. 2 ff.

[7] See A. P. Brogan, "John Locke and Utilitarianism," *Ethics*, LXIX (January, 1959), 79–93.

of the classical tradition. That we here confront a continuum of opinions and not a stark dichotomy can be seen in John Locke's *Some Thoughts concerning Education,* which is based by and large on his antirationalistic empiricism and assumptions as to man's egoism. Yet Locke's two recommendations for educational reading material are the Bible and Cicero's *Offices*[8]—the argument of the latter is precisely against egoistic hedonism (expediency or *utilitas*) in the name of rational virtues worthy to be pursued at the cost even of pain or death.

But in the tradition of John Calvin (and in the philosophy of Hobbes) the possibility of human goodness was almost totally denied. Some of Swift's contemporaries—for example, the Third Earl of Shaftesbury[9]—defended human nature as having not only the potentiality for goodness and virtue, but also the inclination toward them. It is difficult to place Swift in this controversy, as a passage from Part III of *Gulliver's Travels* indicates: In Glubbdubdrib, Gulliver, with the help of sorcerers, talks with three dead kings who:

> . . . protested . . . that in their whole Reigns they did never once prefer any Person of Merit, unless by Mistake or Treachery of some Minister in whom they confided: Neither would they do it if they were to live again; and they shewed with great Strength of Reason, that the Royal Throne could not be supported without Corruption; because, that positive, confident, restive Temper, which Virtue infused into Man, was a perpetual Clog to publick Business. (III, viii, 6)[10]

Does Swift suggest here the possibility of true virtue, courageous and antimonarchic? Or does Swift suggest that some selfishly obdurate idealists are to be condemned for obstructing public policy through their *pretensions* to virtue? If the reader is a Hobbesian, or if he believes that Swift was a Hobbesian, he may take the passage to mean just that.[11]

But if one knows of Swift's constant concern for the injustice of neglected merit, if one knows of his great admiration for haters and destroyers of unjust kings, if one knows of his oft-reiterated belief in the

[8] John Locke, *Works,* 10th ed. (London: Bye and Law, 1801), X, Sections 159, 185.

[9] See his *Inquiry concerning Virtue,* Book II, Part 1.

[10] All citations to *Gulliver's Travels* are made by giving book, chapter, and paragraph numbers. I quote from PW, XI.

[11] Mandeville's irony, for example, often outs on a Hobbesian line. The moral of "The Grumbling Hive" is that "Fools only strive / To make a Great an Honest Hive." Elsewhere Mandeville observes that "all the Virtues together . . . could not possibly be a thousandth Part so serviceable, to make an opulent, powerful, and what we call a flourishing Kingdom" as the vices are. See *The Fable of the Bees,* ed. F. B. Kaye (Oxford: The Clarendon Press, 1924), I, 30, 228. Hobbes' pronouncements on this point are considered in Chapter 8.

principles of classical republicanism,[12] then one can see not only that Swift satirizes the injustice of kings but also that he is having fun with the specious Hobbesian view that public business and public authority are not to be upset by men who pretend to merit, no matter how bad the public authority is. These observations cannot be convincing to Swift's readers and critics unless Swift's belief in the possibility of human excellence can be established.

A similar question is whether Swift joined Pope and other writers of theodicies who used the chain-of-being argument to solve the problem of man's imperfections. Lovejoy has pointed out the consequences of the principle of plenitude when it is applied to moral and social issues: since man is not very high on the scale of being, we cannot ask very much of him.[13] Thus adherents of this view decried Stoicism and all rigorous moral codes as foolish, impossible goals for man. Opposed to this was an old belief in the possibility of heroism, romantic or classical heroism—for example, the heroism of Plutarch's *Lives,* which was so much praised in the Renaissance and the Enlightenment. Was Swift complacent about man's potentialities? Or was he a bit romantic on the subject of a few heroes?

To compound the questions, one could ask whether Swift was a classicist (an ancient) or a modernist, or whether he accepted the world as it is or condemned it from a utopian, idealistic vantage. But the questions would be quickly answered, for it is well known that Swift took the side of the ancients in *The Battle of the Books* and that he ironically noted his (or his creature's) intention to write a panegyric on the world. For these reasons alone, it would seem wise to hesitate before placing Swift in any *modern* posture. And, since of course the world has grown more modern and more modern since Swift's day, it might be well to call a sensitive twentieth-century writer as witness to the distance of our intellectual times from Swift's. Ortega y Gasset explains a twentieth-century predilection which he calls "antiutopianism or antirationalism":

---

[12] See Chapters 4 and 5. Zera S. Fink, who has made a study of classical republicanism in the seventeenth and eighteenth centuries, explains how the basic terms were understood: when writers in those centuries "spoke of a republic, they had in mind a state which was not headed by a king and in which the hereditary principle did not prevail in whole or in part in determining the headship . . . By a 'classical republican' I mean a person who advocated or admired a republic, and took his ideas for such a government in whole or in part from the ancient masterpieces of political organization, their supposed modern-counterparts, or their ancient and modern expositors."—See *The Classical Republicans* (Evanston: Northwestern University Press, 1945), p. x.

[13] Lovejoy's point is discussed in more detail in Chapter 3.

The utopian conception is one which, while believing itself to arise from "nowhere," yet claims to be valid for everyone. . . . Such puerile insubordination to the conditions imposed on us by reality, such incapacity for the cheerful acceptance of destiny, so ingenuous an assumption that it is easy to substitute our own sterile desires, are features of a spirit that is today nearing an end and on the verge of giving place to another completely antagonistic to it. . . .

The utopist aberration of human intelligence begins in Greece and occurs wherever rationalism reaches the point of exacerbation. Pure reason constructs an exemplary world—a physical or political cosmos—in the belief that it is the true reality.[14]

However willing the twentieth century to accept "the conditions imposed on us by reality," Swift was hardly so complacent. The ins and outs of his quarrel with the world, with reality, form the subject matter of the following pages.

[14] José Ortega y Gasset, *The Modern Theme* (New York: Doubleday, 1961), pp. 144–145.

CHAPTER 2

Swift's Debasement of Human Nature

That human beings find the vices a much more zestful and engaging topic than the virtues is as true in our day as in Swift's. It is then discretion to begin with the happier topic, to study that part of Swift's writing which many readers would call the essential or only Swift— that is, to serve up a collection of little pessimistic flowers, an anthology of his indictments of human nature. And Swift's readers seem to have good reason: his creatures, the Yahoos, have especially contributed to his disfavor among lovers of humanity. Captain Gulliver himself notes in the letter to Sympson that he has been accused of "degrading human nature."[1] The disturbing element is the presentation of the Yahoos, Swift explains in his "Panegyric on Dean Swift," in which he lets himself be charged with a number of faults, one of which is that "Gulliver divinely shews, / That Humankind are all Yahoos" (P, II, 498). Many of Swift's comments seem to authenticate the charge:

> I could give Instances Enough
> That Human Friendship is but Stuff. (P, II, 545)

> the Moralist design'd
> A Compliment on Human-Kind:
> For, here he owns, that now and then
> Beasts may degen'rate into Men. (P, II, 608)

> I think you are a little too nice and punctilious for
> a man of this world [he wrote to a friend], and expect
> more from human race than their corruptions can
> afford. (C, IV, 92)

One occasion brings Swift to observe that it is "natural to Mankind to be more violent in an ill Cause than a good one" (PW, VI, 78); and the unauthorized publication of one of his private poems gives him the "ungrateful task of reflecting on the baseness of mankind which I knew sufficiently before" (C, III, 306).

---

[1] Pope and Gay wrote Swift on November 17, 1726, that Bolingbroke had criticized the *Travels* for its depreciation of human nature, C, III, 359.

I

A TUB OF VICE AND A THIMBLEFUL OF VIRTUE

These cynical comments suggest that Swift belongs to the egoistic-hedonic school of Hobbes, La Rochefoucauld, and Mandeville. Some-times Swift clearly assumes that man is a selfish creature forever seeking his own pleasure:

> The Motives of the best Actions will not bear too strict an Enquiry. It is allowed, that the Cause of most Actions, good or bad, may be resolved into the Love of our selves: But the Self-Love of some Men inclines them to please others; and the Self-Love of others is wholly employed in pleasing themselves. This makes the great Distinction between Virtue and Vice. Religion is the best Motive of all Actions; yet Religion is al-lowed to be the highest Instance of Self-Love. (PW, IV, 243; cf. C, III, 430)

Moreover, Swift often gives a Hobbist account of motivation in his sermons: ". . . human nature is so constituted, that we can never pursue any thing heartily but upon hopes of a reward" (PW, IX, 244).

Since Swift was a Christian priest, perhaps his pessimism has doc-trinal as well as experiential grounds—that is, Swift could have been a Calvinist or an Augustinian believing in the doctrine of original sin. In view of *A Tale of a Tub,* no one can speak of Swift as a Calvinist, but it would be instructive if his writings contain affirmations of his adherence to the Augustinian teaching regarding man's innate de-pravity. One such affirmation is a favorite of Swift scholars, to judge by the frequency of its quotation. The sentence, however, is John Arbuthnot's: "I have an opportunity," he wrote to Swift, "calmly and philosophically to consider that treasure of vileness and baseness, that I always believed to be in the heart of man" (C, II, 233). The point of Arbuthnot's letter is that there is one exception to this judgment: the addressee, Jonathan Swift!

In the only place where Swift, in a serious and nonironic way,[2] dis-cusses the Fall and the story of the Garden of Eden, he observes that men, unlike animals, "degenerate every day, merely by the folly, the perverseness, the avarice, the tyranny, the pride, the treachery, the inhumanity of their own kind" (PW, IX, 264). This idea has been

---

[2] Swift wrote Gay (January 8, 1722/23): "Tell me, are you not under original sin by the dedication of your Eclogues to Lord Bolingbroke?" (C, III, 149). How-ever, in the posthumously published *An Evening Prayer* is a rare (if not the only) orthodox reference to "our wicked and corrupt nature" (TS, III, 318).

scouted out by Lovejoy, who designates it a "negative philosophy of history."[3] In Swift's writings this notion of gradual and inevitable decay *after high points of human achievement* seems to be more the poetic or classical picture of degeneration from a Golden Age, or several somewhat-golden ages, than St. Augustine's doctrine of original sin. In an early pamphlet, *Contests and Dissentions in Athens and Rome,* Swift implies that at certain times a people can be noble and virtuous (PW, I, 212), but that it is the nature of human things to decay; he quotes Polybius with approval:

> . . . those Abuses and Corruptions, which in Time destroy a Government, are sown along with the very Seeds of it, and both grow up together: And that, as Rust eats away Iron, and Worms devour Wood; and both are a Sort of Plagues, born and bred along with the Substance they destroy; so with every Form and Scheme of Government that Man can invent, some Vice, or Corruption creeps in with the very Institution, which grows up along with, and at the last destroys it. (PW, I, 217)

Swift's purpose in that pamphlet was nonetheless to put forward a scheme of government which he believed most secure against corruptions. The best explanation of Swift's sentiments of this kind is to be found in a letter to Archbishop King:

> I very much applaud your Grace's sanguine temper, as you call it, and your comparison of religion to paternal affection; but the world is divided into two sects, those that hope the best, and those that fear the worst; your Grace is of the former, which is the wiser, the nobler, and most pious principle; and although I endeavor to avoid being of the other, yet upon this article I have sometimes strange weaknesses. *I compare true religion to learning and civility, which have ever been in the world, but very often shifted their scenes.* (C, I, 130; italics mine)

To twentieth-century ears, saying that one age or place is morally superior or inferior sounds unsophisticated. But the belief that at times there are better men, better countries, which succumb to the gradual corruption of time, informs all Swift's thinking and most of his writings.

Swift's friend William Congreve wrote a poem which occasioned a direct statement by Swift of his views on human achievement in certain times. Congreve anticipated the relativist views of our own century in his "Epistle to Viscount Cobham":

---

[3] Arthur O. Lovejoy, "The Parallel of Deism and Classicism," *Essays in the History of Ideas* (New York: Putnam, 1960), p. 89. First printed in *MP*, XXIX (February, 1932), 281–299.

> Virtue now is neither more or less
> And Vice is only varied in the Dress;
> Believe it, Men have ever been the same,
> And all the Golden Age, is but a Dream.[4]

Swift gave vent to his splenetic disagreement in a letter to Pope and Bolingbroke:

> I have read my friend Congreve's verses to Lord Cobham, which end with a vile and false moral, and I remember is not in [the poem by] Horace to Tibullus which he imitates, that all times are equally virtuous and vicious, wherein he differs from all poets, philosophers, and Christians that ever writ. It is more probable that there may be an equal quantity of virtues always in the world, but sometimes there may be a peck of it in Asia, and hardly a thimbleful in Europe. But if there be no virtue, there is abundance of sincerity; for I will venture all I am worth, that there is not one human creature in power, who will not be modest enough to confess that he proceeds wholly upon a principle of corruption.[5] I say this, because I have a scheme . . . to govern England upon the principles of virtue, and when the nation is ripe for it, I desire you will send for me. I have learned this by living like a hermit, by which I am got backward about nineteen hundred years in the era of the world, and begin to wonder at the wickedness of men. (C, IV, 77)

Although Swift allowed himself the privilege of being cynical about his own era, he resented Congreve's being cynical about earlier human greatness, compared with which the present state of life was degenerate! Significantly, Swift's scheme "to govern England upon the principles of virtue" derives from the height of the Roman Republic (1,900 years before Swift). The response to Congreve's poem reveals the two strongest tendencies of Swift's character: first, a hatred of contemporary vice, and, second, a longing admiration of the all-too-limited amount of human excellence. Swift's readers have usually sensed the one so acutely that they ignore the other.

II

THE SOCIALLY NOXIOUS VICES

Aristotle describes the comic writer as concerned with characters worse than ordinary. Swift the satirist fits the description perfectly, especially when we view his works—for example, *A Tale of a Tub*— as studies in human nonsense and vice. Even his idle pursuits reflect this interest—consider not only the collections of trite expressions and low

---

[4] William Congreve, *The Complete Works of William Congreve*, ed. Montague Sommers, IV (London: Nonesuch, 1923), 178.
[5] See the opinion of "Three Kings" in Part III, *Gulliver's Travels* (III, viii, 6).

neologisms but also the virtuoso catalogs of vices,[6] of which the monumental "muster roll"[7] in "The Voyage to the Land of the Houyhnhnms" is the fullest:

> . . . I did not feel the Treachery or Inconstancy of a Friend, nor the Injuries of a secret or open Enemy. I had no Occasion of bribing, flattering or pimping, to procure the Favour of any great Man, or of his Minion. I wanted no Fence against Fraud or Oppression: Here was neither Physician to destroy my Body, nor Lawyer to ruin my Fortune; No Informer to watch my Words and Actions, or forge Accusations against me for Hire: Here were no Gibers, Censurers, Backbiters, Pickpockets, Highwaymen, House-breakers, Attorneys, Bawds, Buffoons, Gamesters, Politicians, Wits, Spleneticks, tedious Talkers, Controvertists, Ravishers, Murderers, Robbers, Virtuouso's; no Leaders or Followers of Party and Faction; no Encouragers to Vice, by Seducement or Examples: No Dungeon, Axes, Gibbets, Whipping-posts, or Pillories; No cheating Shopkeepers or Mechanicks: No Pride, Vanity or Affectation: No Fops, Bullies, Drunkards, strolling Whores, or Poxes: No ranting, lewd, expensive Wives: No stupid, proud Pedants: No importunate, over-bearing, quarrelsome, noisy, roaring, empty, conceited, swearing Companions: No Scoundrels raised from the Dust upon the Merit of their Vices; or Nobility thrown into it on account of their Virtues: No Lords, Fidlers, Judges or Dancing-masters. (IV, x, 1)

Nearly every frailty of character there represented is socially harmful, obnoxious, or unpleasant; Swift believed all to be the proper target for the satirist and reformer (see PW, VII, 5). And to aim at such is in keeping with the tradition of British ethical philosophy, which regards the problem of social happiness in a way that almost excludes any question of personal excellence or "personality development."

On the basis of the attention that Swift lavishes on them, one can determine what the deadly social sins are: (a) pride, ambition, avarice, luxury; (b) inhumanity (cruelty, revenge, oppression, brutality, malice, insensibility to suffering) and political treachery (false witnessing, insincerity, breach of trust, fraud, faction, informing); and (c) injustice.

a. *Pride, ambition, avarice, luxury.* Swift seems to assume that vice is acting for personal interest (to satisfy personal passion) to the detriment of the public good (PW, II, 9). Since socially beneficial actions usually are based on reasoning or principles[8] (and perhaps also on an inclination to follow reason or principles), selfish-vicious actions come about from the triumph of the passions, or interest, over reason and

---

[6] E.g., see PW, I, 227; IV, 73; VI, 44; VII, 73; VIII, 36; X, 25; XII, 123–124; P, II, 551–552, 724–725.
[7] The term is Sheridan's, p. 443.
[8] See his sermon "Doing Good," PW, IX, 232–240.

principles (PW, VII, 4; VIII, 87; XII, 255). And pride is the name
for the disposition to give egoistic passions full rein. Identical with the
restless acquisitiveness of men, pride takes the form of love of political
power (ambition) and love of money (avarice and the often resultant
luxury): ". . . is Avarice perhaps the same Passion with Ambition,"
Swift asked, "only placed in more ignoble and dastardly Minds; by
which the Object is changed from Power to Money?" (PW, III, 81).
Swift's own contempt of greediness (until his last years) can be best
seen in his refusal to make money on his books,[9] in his insistence that his
printer not make a job of a collected edition of his works, and even in
the provisions of his will, designed to prevent anyone's illegally profiting
by his principal bequest. Swift's attacks on Marlborough's love of
money, while politically motivated, nonetheless reflect Swift's own deepest convictions.

In the matter of burgeoning venality and love of luxury, Swift clearly
opposed the powerful, general current of the time.[10] He wrongly forecast
that "it is altogether impossible for any nation to preserve its liberty long
under a tenth part of the present luxury, infidelity, and a million of
corruptions" (C, V, 143).[11] In admonition, he points to the time "when
the virtue of [Rome] gave place to luxury and ambition" (C, III, 122).
These new developments in England, increased venality and love of
sybaritic living, he identified with incipient competitive capitalism—
"the Bank, East India, and South Sea," the "old Whig measures" (C,
II, 238). His sympathies were all with the landed and with the traditions of England before the rise of modern capitalism. In an *Intelligencer* paper on education he subjects the family life of the newly rich,
or the overrich, to sharp satire, especially the pampering, overdressing,
and spoiling of children.[12] Swift gives the father sound financial senti-

[9] With Pope's help, Swift got £200 for *Gulliver's Travels*. Yet Swift seemed indifferent about the money, which he left in John Gay's possession (Gay was hardly the
most trustworthy of Swift's friends, insofar as caring for money is concerned) until
Gay's death (C, IV, 32, 124, 133, 158, 173, 398–399). Scott was amazed at Swift's
"total indifference to literary fame," (Scott, p. 451). Of course, literary fame and
fortune are near allied.

[10] J. C. Maxwell discovers the basis of Swift's moralism in his disappointments
and maladjustments to his environment, coupled with too great an admiration for
the classics, especially Plutarch's heroes. See "Demigods & Pickpockets: The Augustan Myth in Swift and Rousseau." *Scrutiny*, XI (Summer, 1942), 34–39.

[11] See C, V, 308–309, 316–317, 368, 373, 380, 394. On Swift's attitude toward
luxury, see Louis Landa, *Swift and the Church of Ireland* (Oxford: Clarendon Press,
1954), p. 110; and G. K. Chesterton, *All I Survey* (London: Dodd, Mead, 1933),
pp. 69–70.

[12] The vehemence of Swift's detestation of indulging children so as to ruin their
characters cannot be overstated, as one could perhaps judge from the "utopian"
customs of Lilliput. He wrote to a mother whose favorite child had died: ". . .
favourite children are either spoiled by their parents' indulgence, or soon taken out

ments: "if what is commonly said be true, that Money answereth all Things, why should my Son be honest, temperate, just, or charitable, since he hath no Intention to depend on any of these Qualities for a Maintenance?" Swift goes on to concede with bitter irony that some good comes of the decay of the luxurious—". . . many great Families coming to an End by the Sloth, Luxury, and abandoned Lusts, which enervated their Breed through every Succession, producing gradually a more effeminate Race, wholly unfit for Propagation" (PW, XII, 53).[13]

Thanks to Locke (who had countenanced the unlimited acquisition of wealth as implied in the social agreement to use money) and to far-reaching religious and social developments, the old Christian deadly sin of greed grew more and more respectable in Swift's day. Swift's opposition to the change is clear in two touches in *An Argument against Abolishing Christianity*. The author makes it understood that he will speak only of "nominal Christianity; the other having been for some Time wholly laid aside by general Consent, as utterly inconsistent with our present Schemes of Wealth and Power" (PW, II, 28). The final reason for not abolishing "nominal" Christianity is that stocks might fall "One per Cent," which is "Fifty Times more than ever the Wisdom of our Age thought fit to venture for the Preservation of Christianity" (PW, II, 39).

b. *Inhumanity and political treachery.* Swift's first political pamphlet, *The Contests and Dissentions,* was written in defense of Somers and several other prominent Whigs who were being impeached by the House of Commons for their part in making a treaty; the pamphlet ends with a condemnation of an unfortunate characteristic of popular political actions such as the impeachment—a "Spirit of Cruelty and Revenge, of Malice and Pride, . . . ungovernable Rage and Anger, . . . Injustice, Sophistry, and Fraud" (PW, I, 227). The severity of Swift's satires has worked to create the impression that he was cruel and callous in excoriating misguided people and that he was somewhat cold and

---

of the world, which last is, generally speaking, the lighter punishment of the two" (C, III, 436).

[13] Coleridge rightly recognized this traditionalism in Swift: "Let England be Sir P. Sidney, Shakespeare, Spenser, Milton, Bacon, Harrington, Swift, Wordsworth; and never let the names of Darwin, Johnson, Hume, *furr* it over!—If these too must be England, let them be another England,—or rather let the first be old England, the spiritual, platonic, old England & the second with Locke at the head of the Philosophers & Pope of the poets, with the long list of Priestleys, Payleys [sic] . . . be representative of commercial G. Britain." See *Coleridge on the Seventeenth Century,* ed. R. F. Brinkley (Durham: Duke University Press, 1955), p. 544. The controlling principle which Swift saw in British history is perhaps the crucial human flaw: not a general depravity or corruption after the Fall, but a tendency to degenerate after some order and virtue are achieved.

heartless, at best a kind of Mosaic judge. *Tout comprendre, c'est tout pardonner* comes closer to summarizing the sensibility of our own century than Swift's. He and many of his contemporaries felt that vice (for example, cruelty) deserves the worst, and that it is in the interest of virtue that vice get the worst.

However cold and heartless Swift may seem, his entire career could be regarded as a story of struggles against inhumanity and all the forms of human mistreatment, not of course in any maudlin way; for, as Hawkesworth indicates, all of Swift's acts of charity, benevolence, and philanthropy "did not appear to be the effects of compassion; for, of the soft sympathy with distress that sometimes sparkles in the eye, and sometimes glows upon the Cheek, he shewed no sign, and he may therefore be supposed to have wanted it; however it is certain that he was wholly free from ill nature."[14] Swift's very first political pamphlet and nearly all those he wrote in Ireland are not sentimental bemoanings, but outspoken attacks on assorted forms of cruelty, brutality, malice, and the litigious political activities of ill will which Swift called "faction."[15]

A particular form of malevolence which Swift seems most heartily to have hated, and with good reason, was false witness. After Hobbes had laid such emphasis on the necessity of contract, or trust, in human society—after he had made it, in fact, the third law of nature "that men perform their covenants made"[16]—conservative writers like Swift and Berkeley[17] were perhaps influenced to attach almost ultimate importance to good faith, candor, openhearted dealing, sincerity, faithful witnessing, and the keeping of one's word. Also, after a period of great civil unrest and religious controversy and persecution, the extent to which honest dealing is essential in a society becomes much more apparent. Swift devoted a sermon to the evil of "False Witness" (PW, IX, 180–189). He was unceasing in hating "the whole tribe of informers, the most accursed and prostitute and abandoned race that God ever permitted to plague mankind" (C, III, 121).

Swift believed that party politics had destroyed that natural amity which had existed earlier in English social and political life; he makes this loss a secondary theme of his sermon on "Brotherly Love" (PW, IX, 171–179). The most objectionable instances of political hostility occurred whenever the administration changed hands, those relieved of

[14] Hawkesworth, p. 62.
[15] See, e.g., P, II, 725; PW, IV, 73; VIII, 56; X, 25; TS, X, 202–214, 236.
[16] *Leviathan*, XV (93).
[17] See Berkeley's brief pamphlet, "Passive Obedience," *The Works of George Berkeley*, ed. A. A. Luce and T. E. Jessop (Edinburgh: T. Nelson, 1948–1957), VI, 17–46.

office becoming the prey of their successors, to suffer attainder, perhaps death, or (mercifully) only general obloquy. Swift took part in a transfer of power and dealt heavy-handedly with the reputations of the Whigs newly out of office. Yet, if we can believe the *Journal to Stella,* he stood for moderation: of the Tory ministry's treatment of Marlborough he wrote, "I do not love to see personal resentment mix with public affairs" (J, II, 453). And he believed that he had "hindered many a bitter thing against [Marlborough], not for his own sake, but because I thought it looked base" (J, II, 597).[18]

It seemed to Swift that cruelty was no part of Harley's nature; and he praised the Lord Treasurer for the "goodness of his Humour, and agreeable Conversation," and found him a "firm Friend, and a placable Enemy" (PW, VII, 75; III, 79). In other words, to Swift, Harley was a rarity, a perfectly tamed politician; and it is proof, I think, of Swift's feelings against revenge, and of the justness of his estimate of Harley, that the change of ministry which brought Harley to head the government was a transfer of power both complete and peaceful. Compared to the change which brought in the Whigs in 1714, it was moderate and merciful.

The case was altered when, after the death of Queen Anne, Lord Wharton headed the secret committee of inquiry (namely, the Whig committee for revenge): Oxford was imprisoned; Ormonde, Bolingbroke, Atterbury were exiled. The second and third volumes of Ball's edition of Swift's correspondence are a record of his bitter reactions to those reprisals, taken partly for that crime, the Peace of Utrecht. "It is a wonderful thing to see the Tories provoking his present Majesty," he wrote with irony of George I, "whose clemency, mercy, and forgiving temper, have been so signal, so extraordinary, so more than humane, during the whole course of his reign" (C, III, 141). Pope was later to quote, with reference to the second George, "Praise undeserved is scandal in disguise."

A greater and more lasting instance of cruelty soon engaged Swift's attention: the wholesale oppression of the Irish:

A great cause of [Ireland's] Misery, is the Aegyptian Bondage of cruel, oppressing, covetous Landlords, expecting that all who live under them should make Bricks without Straw, who grieve and envy when they see a Tenant of their own in a whole Coat, or able to afford one comfortable Meal in a Month, by which the Spirits of the People are broken, and made for Slavery; the Farmers and Cottagers, almost through the whole Kingdom, being to all Intents and Purposes as real Beggars, as

18 That is, not for a Christian, but a pagan, reason.

any of those to whom we give out Charity in the Streets. And these cruel Landlords are every Day unpeopling their Kingdom, by forbidding their miserable Tenants to till the Earth, against common Reason and Justice, and contrary to the Practice and Prudence of all other Nations. (PW, IX, 201)

Swift spent most of his life serving the interests of Ireland, in one way or another; and, if one (like his early biographers) is not misled by the cynical manner he assumed at times, one can clearly see that he spent those years in mainly futile efforts to discourage England from further depredations and to encourage the Irish to improve their own lot. The only full account of Swift's efforts against oppression and cruelty in Ireland is in the highly commendatory biography by William Sheridan (whose book Dr. Johnson unjustly damned). Sheridan, an Irishman (and therefore much more apt to recognize a benefactor of Ireland than a modern American or British scholar), tells a long and sad story (not really dull, only repetitive), of which *A Modest Proposal* is not even the finale, however fraught with despair and hatred of inhumanity it may be. *A Modest Proposal* is something like the climax of the story; and even after it, Swift continued to exhort the Irish and to excoriate the British.

A Modest Proposal is actually the proof of Swift's humanity, as is clear to anyone who reads all his correspondence. It is a masterpiece of irony, which presents the question in a crucial way: is the text enough, without the long, sad story behind it? Can one paragraph represent to the reader the active charity and the sustained opposition to cruelty and oppression which inspired the satire?

I desire the Reader will observe, that I calculate my Remedy for this one individual Kingdom of Ireland, and for no other that ever was, is, or I think ever can be upon Earth. Therefore, let no man talk to me of other Expedients: Of taxing our Absentees at five Shillings a Pound: Of using neither Cloaths, nor Houshold Furniture except what is of our own Growth and Manufacture: Of utterly rejecting the Materials and Instruments that promote foreign Luxury: Of curing the Expensiveness of Pride, Vanity, Idleness, and Gaming in our Women: Of introducing a Vein of Parsimony, Prudence and Temperance: Of learning to love our Country, wherein we differ from Laplanders, and the Inhabitants of Topinamboo: Of quitting our Animosities, and Factions; nor act any longer like the Jews, who were murdering one another at the very Moment their City was taken: Of being a little cautious not to sell our Country and Consciences for nothing: Of teaching Landlords to have, at least, one Degree of Mercy towards their Tenants. Lastly, Of putting a Spirit of Honesty, Industry, and Skill into our Shopkeepers; who, if a Resolution could now be taken to buy only our native Goods, would immediately unite to cheat and exact upon us in the Price, the Measure, and the Goodness; nor could ever yet be brought to make one fair Proposal of just Dealing, though often and earnestly invited to it. (PW, XII, 116–117)

The history of the criticism of *A Modest Proposal* is proof that for most readers the text is not enough, not even to prevent an author's getting a reputation the opposite of the truth, that of a savage misanthrope whose imagination was pleased to think of serving up a young child "fricaseed."[19] A life time of condemning inhumanity is called misanthropy!

c. *Injustice*.   The problem of injustice is always, to Swift, the problem of neglected merit or mistreated merit. It forms the dominant theme in his correspondence, and I would judge hatred of injustice to be the most prominent trait of his character. His letters are full of ironies on "this exploded custom of rewarding merit" and invective against politicians who can, but do not, help the talented and deserving (C, I, 287, 291). He wonders at Addison's being both qualified and successful in politics (C, II, 395). He reasons that men of great talents so seldom get what they deserve because ordinary people envy them so much (C, III, 41–42). And he complains, on too many occasions to count, of his recommendations of deserving people which have no effect:

> [I] have once or twice recommended persons to you [he wrote to Bishop Stearne, who got his bishopric in order that the deanery he left could be given to Swift], who are no relations or friends of mine, but merely for their general good character, which availed so little, that those very persons had the greatest share of your neglect. I then gave over all thoughts of being instrumental to place merit and virtue under your protection by my recommendations. (C, V, 17)[20]

III

PRIVATE IMPERFECTIONS

For a clergyman Swift had little to say about virtues which make up personal excellence and which have little to do with social relationships. For example, he pays little attention to unchastity, intemperance, or impiety (in the sense of a Christian's failure to achieve complete faith

---

[19] Writing against two bills pending before the Irish parliament, Swift makes a remark worthy a disciple of La Rochefoucauld: "There are no Qualities more incident to the Frailty and Corruptions of human Kind, than an Indifference, or Insensibility for other Mens Sufferings, and a sudden Forgetfulness of their own former humble State, when they rise in the World." But he goes on to add a sentiment one would expect from a Benevolist: such things *"naturally* should seem to operate a quite contrary Way" (PW, XII, 191; italics mine).

[20] See also C, I, 119; II, 72; III, 46, 118, 249; IV, 144; V, 170, 171; J, II, 659.

or regeneration).[21] Yet, for cowardice, which he regarded mainly as a purely personal weakness, he had the greatest contempt. On this point his disagreement with Hobbes is absolute, for Hobbes had discovered all the motive force behind man's rational construction of society in the fear of death and pain. Fearfulness is the essence of man, according to Hobbes, and therefore cannot be considered vicious. His definition of courage is significant: the "hope of avoiding . . . hurt by resistance"[22]— not an indifference to death or the fear of something greater than death, there being, for Hobbes, no greater evil than death. One of Swift's "Thoughts on Various Subjects" holds no such complacent view of cowards:

> It is unwise to punish Cowards with Ignominy; for if they had regarded that, they would not have been Cowards: Death is their proper Punishment, because they fear it the most. (PW, I, 242)

In his list of "those who have made a mean contemptible Figure" Swift includes primarily examples of cowardice, craven braggadocio, and lack of will power to live up to principles of honor, under threat of violence or death (PW, V, 85–86).

IV

THE FOLLIES OF THE INTELLECT

Swift's satire aimed at intellectual as well as moral frailties. *Folly* and *imprudence* were to him terms with as definite meanings as *cowardice* and *injustice*. What folly meant to Swift can best be seen in a rare case, that of a person whom Swift thought to be possessed of a good nature without good sense. Gilbert Burnet, Bishop of Salisbury, was, according to Swift, a fool with good impulses, whose folly was his conviction that the dissenters were rather a good lot and his obliviousness to the threat to society posed by them (PW, V, 266–294). Moreover,

---

[21] A constant idea in his *Thoughts* is that "in the Day of Judgment there will be small Allowance given to the Wise for their want of Morals, or to the Ignorant for their want of Faith; because, both are without Excuse. This renders the Advantages equal of Ignorance and Knowledge. But some Scruples in the Wise, and some Vices in the Ignorant, will perhaps be forgiven upon the Strength of Temptation to each" (PW, I, 243). In his later *Thoughts on Religion* the recurring motifs are that personal scruples of faith are to be kept private and that the publishing of them is the fault to be avoided: ". . . in a country already Christian, to bring so fundamental a point of faith [as the divinity of Christ] into debate, can have no consequences that are not pernicious to morals and public peace" (PW, IX, 262; see also C, III, 247). In his "Introduction" to Ball's edition of Swift's *Correspondence*, J. H. Bernard (Dean of St. Patrick's in the early years of this century) says, "The tendency of [Swift's] 'practical view' of Christianity was to place character and conduct before creed" (C, I, liv).

[22] *Leviathan*, VI (34). See also Michael Oakeshott's discussion of Hobbes's thought in his edition of *Leviathan* (Oxford: Blackwell, 1960), p. xxxvi.

Burnet was something of a zealot, an enthusiast, or a gnostic in religion. That is to say he stressed the primacy of direct inspiration or zeal over common sense, experience, and traditional belief.[23] Swift gave the natural history of gnostic zeal, or "madness," in his coruscating early work, *A Tale of a Tub*. His opinion never varied to the end of his career:

> ... no Opinions are maintained with so much Obstinacy as those in Religion, especially by such Zealots who never bore the least Regard to Religion, Conscience, Honour, Justice, Truth, Mercy, or common Morality, farther than in outward Appearance; under the Mask of Hypocrisy, to promote their diabolical Designs. And, therefore, Bishop Burnet, one of their Oracles, tells us honestly, that the Saints of those Fanatick Times, pronounced themselves above Morality, which they reckoned among beggarly Elements; but the Meaning of those two last Words thus applied, we confess to be above our Understanding. (PW, XII, 289)

Consequently Swift regarded as pernicious the influence of the freethinkers and Quakers, whose individual preferences themselves were not wrong, but their publication and practice, which might encourage behavior contrary to the traditional, the conventional, the common. To Swift, a freethinker is like a madman, one who speaks his mind without thought of the consequences. And if freethinkers (a term that Swift used to include Deists) publish their thoughts "to the world, they ought to be answerable for the effects their thoughts produce upon others" (PW, IV, 49).[24] The wise course is one of caution:

> The Humour of exploding many Things under the Names of Trifles, Fopperies, and only imaginary Goods, is a very false Proof either of Wisdom or Magnanimity; and a great Check to virtuous Actions. (PW, IV, 244)

One could, for example, easily explode the notion of fame:

> It requires but little Philosophy to discover and observe that there is no intrinsick Value in [fame]; however, if it be founded in our Nature, as an Incitement to Virtue, it ought not to be ridiculed. (PW, IV, 244)

The Quaker's refusal to take oaths is a foolish singularity, pernicious to a common form which is very useful, at least as a nod to that sincerity

---

[23] On gnosticism in the seventeenth century, see Eric Voegelin, *The New Science of Politics* (Chicago: University of Chicago Press, 1952), pp. 133 ff. On Swift's attitude toward gnosticism, see Ronald Paulson, *Theme and Structure in Swift's Tale of a Tub* (New Haven: Yale University Press, 1960), pp. 98 ff.

[24] To modern readers this sounds like totalitarian thought-control. But in Swift's day enlightenment had not proceeded to the point that all opinions were equal, or that intelligence was exactly dubiety regarding the truth of all opinions. There was still believed to be a right and a wrong opinion, right in terms of considerations or reasons.

vital to public order (PW, VII, 106–109). And it is folly to preach against atheists from the pulpit, since doing so merely brings into question what it is useless to answer (PW, IX, 77–78).

Wit, learning, or science, too, while in themselves good, can degenerate into folly. To set up as wit or scholar without any claim to merit, or a very small claim, stirred Swift's and his friend Pope's indignation.[25] But worse is to pursue any form of knowledge to the exclusion of all humanity and common morality. Swift's attitude is properly that of the gentleman, or man of honor, and perhaps there is a hint as to the source of Swift's thinking in the fact that in an "Ode to Sir William Temple" he first inveighs against the "Heresy . . . That Knowledge forfeits all Humanity" (P, I, 28). An extreme case of such forfeiture can be found in the career of an unfortunate "scientist," who would have been at home in the Academy of Lagado; part of his madness is revealed in Swift's and Arbuthnot's correspondence:

> A projector has lately applied to me [Swift wrote Archbishop King] to recommend him to the Ministry about an invention for finding out the longitude. He has given in a petition to the Queen by Mr. Secretary St. John. I understand nothing of the mathematics; but I am told it is a thing as improbable as the philosopher's stone, or perpetual motion. (C, I, 324–325)

> Whiston has at last published his project of the longitude [Arbuthnot wrote Swift]; the most ridiculous thing that ever was thought on. But a pox on him! he has spoiled one of my papers of Scriblerus, which was a proposal for the longitude, not very unlike his, to this purpose: that since there was no pole for East and West, that all the Princes of Europe should join and build two prodigious poles, upon high mountains, with a vast light-house to serve for a pole-star. I was thinking of a calculation of the time, charges, and dimensions. Now you must understand, his project is by light-houses, and explosion of bombs at a certain hour. (C, II, 186)

> It was a malicious satire of yours upon Whiston [Swift replies], that what you intended as a ridicule, should be any way struck upon by him for a reality. (C, II, 197)

Besides his sober mathematical projects, William Whiston (1667–1752) engaged in religious controversy. He adhered to the Arian heresy, and was therefore deprived of his Cambridge lectureship. He planned to build a model of the tabernacle of Moses, lectured on the coming of the Messiah and the return of the Jews to Israel, and foretold the millennium, *anno* 1766.

Swift's objections were not solely against applied science or pro-

---

[25] Notably in *A Tale of a Tub* and *The Dunciad.*

jectors; pure or theoretical science could be nonhumane. His friend Sheridan was (Swift felt) a man of good nature, who neglected his own interests on account of his speculation. By Swift's account, Sheridan was "a man of intent and abstracted thinking, enslaved by mathematics" (C, III, 268).

Swift was completely convinced of the necessity for fixed, stabilized opinions, rooted in common thought and common forms. It is often believed that Swift was a sceptic at heart, that he saw human reason as radically limited.[26] But his scepticism applies to the bolder flights of reason and to the efficacy of dialectic. On basic points, such as the necessity for religion and the certainty of some few primary ethical principles, he had no doubt. That is to say, his scepticism leads not to liberalism or positivism, but to dogmatism, by which I mean not that Swift felt absolute security in his beliefs (as he may well have), but that he recognized that a fixed, unchallenged opinion in religion and morals is indispensable for social order. It should be noted that Bishop Berkeley, a close reasoner of great fame, adopted much the same point of view: the purpose of his "idealism" was to get rid, once and for all, of the causes of scepticism;[27] his moral philosophy is much more inflexible than Swift's.[28] Just as Swift hoped to ridicule some freethinkers out of at least their inclination to publish their views, so Berkeley hoped to put the quietus to attacks on morals and religion which he felt were generated out of certain theoretical errors in the materialistic world view then growing up with natural science.

In Swift's mind a clear-cut, rigid simplicity was best: in language, "Simplicity . . . is one of the greatest Perfections" (PW, IV, 15), "Simplicity, without which no human Performance can arrive to any great Perfection, is no where more eminently useful than in" preaching (PW, IX, 68); and in morals, "It is your business," Swift wrote to a younger contemporary, "who are coming into the world, to put a stop to these corruptions, and recall that simplicity which in everything of value ought to be followed" (C, V, 113).

Often Swift seems to express the view of the man of the world, the pragmatist, who has no patience with abstractions or theories which are

[26] This is further discussed in Chapter 7. Consider in this connection the fideistic tradition in the seventeenth century, which Louis Bredvold has studied in *The Intellectual Milieu of John Dryden* (Ann Arbor: University of Michigan Press, 1956, paperback reissue).
[27] This is clear in the subtitle of *The Principles of Human Knowledge*—"Wherein the chief causes of error and difficulty in the Sciences, with the grounds of Scepticism, Atheism, and Irreligion, are inquired into"—and in Paragraph No. 155. It is a constant theme in his writings, especially in *Alciphron*.
[28] Consider the absolute moral doctrine he expounds in "Passive Obedience."

belied by everyday experience. Thus, on public and private levels, he condemns those who follow speculative principles to their own detriment. Faced with the problem of convincing the public of the necessity of peace, after the years and years of war over the Spanish succession, Swift had to refute those who argued that England was bound by principles of honor to stand by her allies. To a surprising degree, his techniques in educating the English public of the basic fact of diplomacy have been paralleled recently by statesmen and news commentators, who feel the need to convince mainly idealistic liberals that foreign affairs are not games of cricket. England, Swift argued, could afford no such "Romantick disposition" toward her allies, for that would be against "Prudence, or common Reason"—in short, against "our own Interest." "General Speculative Reasons," such as the honor to be won in war, have no force when opposed by considerations for the common good of the nation; and the dishonorable behavior of England's allies had been sufficiently sobering. In view of the American zeal for unconditional surrender in World War II, the following still has significance:

> . . . our Victories only served to lead us on to farther visionary Prospects; advantage was taken of the Sanguin Temper, which so many Successes had wrought the Nation up to; new Romantick Views were proposed, and the old, reasonable, sober Design, was forgot.[29]

Of the same kind, on the private level, are those religious zealots who engage in the romantic knight-errantry of foolish martyrdom (PW, IV, 80). Consider the caricature of this kind of zeal in *A Tale of a Tub:* Jack, representing Calvinism, stands on the streets and begs for slaps, kicks, and blows from every passer-by. He then presents himself at home, badly beaten, a warrior against evil forces:

> Neighbours mine, this broken Head deserves a Plaister; had poor Jack been tender of his Noddle, you would have seen the Pope and the French King, long before this time of Day, among your Wives and your Ware-houses. Dear Christians, the Great Mogul was come as far as White-Chappel, and you may thank these poor Sides that he hath not (God bless us) already swallowed up Man, Woman, and Child. (PW, I, 126)[30]

Swift's attitude toward eccentric individualism is, however, somewhat equivocal: often he speaks with respect of those who act on speculative

---

[29] PW, VI, 9, 15, 20, 24, 36, 48.
[30] This perennial flourishes today: the rightist species, which is ever alone, saving the country from its enemies, who are, variously, Catholics, Jews, Negroes, Comunists.

principles of morality, and even admits that he himself does: ". . . this proposal [a recommendation of an acquaintance for some preferment] of mine is more suitable to the corruptions of the times, than to my own speculative notions of virtue" (C, V, 171–172). Consider, too, his praise of George Berkeley, whose principles could be seen to act against his "interest." Swift wrote to Harley's son that Berkeley "is a true philosopher and an excellent scholar, but of very visionary virtue, and is endeavouring to quit a thousand pounds a year for a hundred at Bermudas [where Berkeley hoped to found a college for the New World]" (C, III, 262) ; and to Lord Carteret:

> I humbly entreat your Excellency, either to use such persuasions as will keep *one of the first men in this kingdom for learning and virtue* quiet at home, or assist him by giving your credit, to compass his romantic design, which, however, is very noble and generous, and directly proper for a great person of your excellent education to encourage. (C, III, 213; italics mine)

The tension in Swift's thinking results from his admiration of the noble and the great, who act for principle against interest, and from his distaste for the neglect of one's own well-being or the well-being of society. A harmony does not always exist between the admirable and the (socially or selfishly) necessary, as can best be seen in the cases of remarkable public servants, who despite their great talents often fail to take the best care of their own and public interests:

> I take the Infelicity of such extraordinary Men to have been caused by their Neglect of Common Forms, together with the Contempt of little Helps, and little Hindrances; which is made by Hobbes[31] the Definition of Magnanimity; and this Contempt, as it certainly displeases the People in generall, so it giveth Offence to all with whom such Ministers have to deal; For, I never yet knew a Minister, who was not earnestly desirous to have it thought, that the Art of Government was a most profound Science: wheras it requires no more in reality, than Diligence, Honesty, and a moderate Share of plain naturall Sense. And therefore men thus qualifyed may very reasonably and justly think, that the Business of the World is best brought about by Regularity and Forms, wherein themselves excell. For, I have frequently observed more Causes of Discontent arise from the Practice of some refined Ministers, to act in common Business, out of the common Road, than from all the usuall Topicks of Displeasure against Men in Power: It is the same thing in other Scenes of Life, and among all Societies or Communities; where no Men are better trusted, or have more success in Business, than those who with some Honesty and a moderate Portion of Understand-

---

[31] *Leviathan,* VI (35).

ing are strict Observers of Time, Place, and Method; and on the Contrary, nothing is more apt to expose Men to the Censure and Obloquy of their Colleagues and the Publick, than a Contempt or Neglect of these Circumstances, however attended with a superiour Genius, and an equall Desire of doing Good. (PW, VIII, 138–139)

But Swift's attitude toward magnanimity of this kind is not disapproval; one of the maxims he taught Vanessa was that "common Forms were not design'd / Directors to a noble Mind" (P, II, 706). And to a statesman who he thought had ignored common forms to his own political destruction, Harley, Swift wrote the following lines:

> Virtue, to crown her Fav'rites, loves to try
> Some new unbeaten Passage to the Sky;
> Where Jove a Seat among the Gods will give
> To those who die, for meriting to live. (P, I, 210) [32]

Patriotic men of great abilities, impelled by their genius and good will and by their virtue, venture out of the beaten paths. The men in English history whom Swift admired were all more or less the victims of their own high principles or great abilities in their controversies, usually with those whom Swift regarded as dunces or knaves. Nearly all these men were of great political eminence and intellectual capacity: Sir Thomas More, Sir Walter Raleigh, the first Earl of Clarendon, Archbishop Laud, the first Earl of Strafford, the first Earl of Shaftesbury, the second Duke of Buckingham, Oxford, and Bolingbroke.[33] Not all were in his opinion unequivocally good, but the strange feature in their careers was that their outstanding virtues (abilities or powers) seemed to have precipitated their misfortune. Swift's reading of the problem of the good or gifted man in a bad world seems to have been the same as the Earl of Oxford's, on a maudlin occasion:

> To serve with love
>   And shed your blood,
> Approved is above.
>   But here below
> Th' examples show,
>   'Tis fatal to be good. (C, II, 199; italics mine) [34]

---

[32] See also Deane Swift, pp. 250–251.

[33] PW, VIII, 138–139; XII, 39; XIII, 123; C, III, 41–42.

[34] See also C, III, 30, 42, 117, 137; I, 117; II, 10. The first *sextumvirate* to appear in Swift's writings were all persecuted for what Swift thought a good action (PW, I, 206–208). And, too, we should remember the case of Sir William Temple, who retired to avoid the slings and arrows of Charles II's reign. See also Swift's remarks on how men of virtue are discouraged from entering public life (PW, I, 224).

CHAPTER 3

The Treasury of Human Worth

Swift's pessimism and misanthropy take an interesting form. Condemning human behavior generally, he yet respects and admires a few patriotic, talented men. Dr. Johnson noticed this peculiarity in Swift (and his friends):

> From the letters that pass between him and Pope, it might be inferred that they, with Arbuthnot and Gay, had engrossed all the understanding and virtue of mankind; that their merits filled the world, or that there was no hope of more. They show the age involved in darkness, and shade the picture with sullen emulation.[1]

To admire only a few and to condemn, in stinging satire, all the rest is to acquire enemies a plenty. And such enemies soon accuse the satirist of finding no goodness at all in mankind. In his own lifetime Swift earned a reputation for denying the existence of human virtue. Since a long tradition has perpetuated that reputation, it is necessary to trace the main arguments of the tradition and to discover whether in fact Swift did believe that virtues exist, before analyzing his praise of assorted virtues.

I

LOWERED ETHICAL GOALS *and* LACERATED HEART?

In 1714[2] an anonymous writer (who may have been Steele or one of Steele's friends) made Swift out to be a Hobbesian or Mandevillian egoist or cynic in a pamphlet entitled *Essays Divine, Moral, and Political: By the Author of the "Tale of a Tub."* The essays are supposedly the self-revelations of Swift; but the purpose of the true author is revealed in the epigraph on the title page: "Out of thy own Mouth will condemn Thee, O Thou Hypocrit." The first three essays, the "Divine" ones, make up "Swift's confessions" of religious infidelity and hypocrisy

---

[1] Johnson's *Life*, pp. 271–272.
[2] The same year Mandeville published *The Fable of the Bees*. His poem "The Grumbling Hive" was first published in 1705.

and general profligacy (pp. 1–22). The "Moral" essays follow: "Swift" begins by defining virtue as "an Essential Good, by which all the Affections in the Possessor tend to the Good of the Publick, without Suffering any Selfish Consideration exclusive of the Publick to interfer" (p. 26). He announces his purpose:

> . . . my Business is, at present, to prove, That there's nothing which is call'd Virtue, as practis'd in the World, but proceeds from the very Source which is opposite to the Being of Virtue, I mean from Self-Interest, or a Personal Regard. (pp. 26–27)

He proceeds to explode the cardinal virtues (justice, fortitude, temperance, prudence) and chastity as things imaginary and nonexistent. His method of argument is clear from his summarizing statement:

> From what I have said already, on the foregoing Heads, which are call'd, The Cardinal Virtues, it's plainly apparent, That there is no such Thing, but that they consist mearly in the Name. And if we should examine the Subordinate Virtues to these, such as Probity, Gratitude, Humility, Patience, Generosity, Modesty, &c. we shall find them all Springing from one of the following Heads, either from Vanity, Ambition, or Self-Interest. (p. 32)

"Swift" gives friendship the same treatment:

> The Idea of it was always Great and Pleasing in the Imagination. It did well enough in the Theory, but made a scurvy Figure in the Practise: The Reason is, that Self is generally concern'd; and that Dear Thing Self, commonly surmounts the Virtue, however Great and Heroic in appearance; not but there is such a Thing as Seeming Friendship in the World. (p. 34)

The last essays, the "Political" ones, are designed to reveal that in his political behavior Swift always acts "in Compliance to the Times, and my Interest, which, is much more valuable to me, than the Good of my Country" (p. 64).

The author of the 1714 *Essays* put in explicit and satiric form what benevolist and romantic readers in the eighteenth and nineteenth centuries came to assume, the intensity of aversion tending to increase as the years passed.[3] As in many other presuppositions and aesthetic biases, critics in our own day have been schooled by Coleridge, who put the Benevolist-Romantic argument in a forward-looking form:

> In Swift's writings there is a false misanthropy grounded upon an exclusive contemplation of the vices and follies of mankind, and this misanthropic tone is also disfigured or brutalized by his obtrusion of physi-

[3] See D. M. Berwick, "The Reputation of Jonathan Swift 1781–1882" (Philadelphia: Princeton, 1941).

cal dirt and coarseness . . . he gives the misanthropic ideal of man—
that is, a being virtuous from rule and duty, but untouched by the principle of love.
Critics in general complain of the Yahoos; I complain of the Houyohn-
hnms.[4]

These remarks contain the germ of a good part of modern pronouncements on Swift—who overlooked the nobler elements in human nature;
whose "vision" is curiously negative; whose thinking is not illuminated
by a principle of love; whose ethical principles are unsatisfactory. The
addendum to the personal attack is the comment on Swift's creatures,
the Houyhnhnms, who are repulsive to Coleridge.

Herbert Read argues that Swift was blind to the high sublime in
human beings, that he wrongfully followed the sceptical cynicism of La
Rochefoucauld. Swift's and La Rochefoucauld's inadequacies are best
revealed if we compare them to Vauvenargues, who was sensible of the
grandeur d'âme, to which man can succeed.[5] F. R. Leavis finds Swift's
irony to be finally negative; Swift deals with values and emotions in such
a way that there is denigration all around, with perhaps only vapid
affirmation; this technique, which is accidental rather than intentional,
results in what I would call "dead-end indirections," or a kind of frus-
tration, to use the term applied by another recent critic.[6] Leavis'
criticism is but a sophistication of Coleridge's: that Swift assails vices
while overlooking the virtues or while adumbrating positives which we
today cannot accept. Since we cannot accept them, Swift did not mean
them, or meant them only vapidly. Thus we have in his satire only a
rather disappointing, destructive technique.[7]

An increasingly popular critical fashion, with regard to Swift's belief
or lack of belief in human goodness, is one instituted about forty years
ago: that Swift took a traditional line regarding man's imperfections,

---

[4] Coleridge's Miscellaneous Criticism, ed. T. M. Raysor (Cambridge, Mass.: Harvard University Press, 1936), pp. 128–130.

[5] Herbert Read, The Sense of Glory (Cambridge: University Press, 1929), pp.
96–99. Almost the same view is taken by George Orwell, Shooting an Elephant (New
York: Harcourt, Brace, 1950), p. 75; and by Caroline Goad, Horace in the English
Literature of the Eighteenth Century (New Haven: Yale University Press, 1918),
p. 172. G. B. Harrison thinks that Swift is too pessimistic to be a political thinker of
any worth: "Jonathan Swift," The Social & Political Ideas of Some English Thinkers in the Augustan Age, ed. F. J. C. Hearnshaw (London: C. G. Harrap, 1928),
p. 208.

[6] Ellen D. Leyburn, "Certain Problems of Allegorical Satire in Gulliver's Travels,"
Huntington LQ, XIII (February, 1950), 189. A. E. Dyson thinks Swift's satire is a
kind of masochistic exhibitionism: "Swift is publicly torturing himself and the
species." See "Swift: The Metamorphosis of Irony," Essays and Studies, n.s., XI
(1958), 65.

[7] F. R. Leavis, The Common Pursuit (London: Chatto & Windus, 1952), pp.
74–87.

an attitude given full expression by St. Augustine, and reasserted in the Renaissance in the form of Montaigne's sceptical humanism.[8] Thus Swift is a Christian realist in morals,[9] believing that human excellence and perfection are but vain ideas,[10] that "perfection among men is, therefore, totally irrelevant, since nature allots certain vices in any case."[11]

These conclusions do not yield the argument to the Benevolists, the defenders of human nature; rather they are the means to a higher praise of Swift, whose reputation suffered from the imputations of the Benevolists. What the Benevolists said was accurate, but the frame of values was wrong. Freed from any sanguinity about human progress, we are sober enough today to accept Swift's pessimism as a legitimate Christian attitude. Swift and his beliefs are not reprehensible. He is just an Augustinian Christian, who "never believed that rational benevolence or action for the good of the species was possible for fallen humanity."[12] Louis Landa has carried this line of apologetics a step farther; for him, Swift becomes the defender of Christian moral theory, threatened by false systems of morals which ignore original sin:

> Swift sensed the danger to orthodox Christianity from an ethical system or any view of human nature stressing man's goodness or strongly asserting man's capacity for virtue. He had no faith in the existence of the benevolent man of Shaftesbury and the anti-Hobbists, the proud, magnanimous man of the Stoics, or the rational man of the deists; his man is a creature of the passions, of pride and self-love, a frail and sinful being in need of redemption.[13]

Overreacting against the condemnation of Swift by Jeffrey and Thackeray in the nineteenth century, the primary motivation of much modern criticism has been an impulse to praise Swift. Thus a scholar

---

[8] T. O. Wedel, "On the Philosophical Background of Gulliver's Travels," *SP*, XXIII (October, 1926), 434–450. Ernest Bernbaum had earlier placed Swift in the "classical-Christian" tradition, which views man as "a being with a *capacity* for spiritual and rational life, but with animal propensities which too often frustrate his fulfillment thereof." Bernbaum further understands Swift's ethical doctrine as a compromise between the extremes of optimistic altruism (as in Shaftesbury and the Deists) and pessimistic egoism (as in Lucretius and Hobbes). See "Introduction" to *Gulliver's Travels* (New York: Harcourt, 1920), pp. viii–x.

[9] Ricardo Quintana, *The Mind and Art of Jonathan Swift* (London: Oxford University Press, 1953), pp. 65–70.

[10] H. M. Dargan, "The Nature of Allegory as Used by Swift," *SP*, XIII (July, 1916), 178.

[11] Samuel Kliger, "The Unity of *Gulliver's Travels*," *MLQ*, VI (December, 1945), 414.

[12] Kathleen Williams, *Jonathan Swift and the Age of Compromise* (Lawrence: University of Kansas Press, 1958), p. 216.

[13] Louis Landa, "Jonathan Swift," *English Institute Essays 1946* (New York: Columbia University Press, 1947), pp. 34–35.

like Landa will enhance Swift's reputation by pitting him as the defender of Augustinian Christianity against the neopagans, while giving the following psychological interpretation of Swift's persistent acts of charity: "I suggest that a simple humanitarian desire to aid his fellowman is a sufficient explanation and one consistent with his character."[14]

The respectable academic opinion of Swift today is that he was a man of "profound orthodoxy"[15]—that is, some kind of traditional Christian —and a man of good sense and good nature (or a man of virtue). Thus he is a virtuous man believing in the impossibility of virtue.[16] The following example is but typical of the pattern often repeated in Swift scholarship, as is that of Landa above. A recent student of Swift's relationship with Addison and Steele (who were at least more benevolist than Swift) first points out that Swift's "insistence on our 'corrupt nature' and his rejection of any system that man has a natural capacity for virtue are inseparable from his conviction of the reality of the Fall."[17] But the same study includes a proof of Swift's high-mindedness (his virtue) in the break with Addison and Steele and his subsequent alignment with Harley: both "are firmly grounded in his refusal in these years to sacrifice his convictions for the sake of political expedience."[18]

It is worthwhile to pause and compare this trend in modern criticism with its beginnings in the 1714 *Essays,* where three charges were brought against Swift: (1) that he was an unbelieving hypocrite in religion, (2) that he neither believed in the possibility of virtue nor was virtuous himself, (3) that in politics he acted solely for selfish reasons. Modern critics hurry to deny the first of these, and occasionally the third. As for the second, they often imply that Swift acted virtuously on occasion; but only a demurrer is entered with reference to his attitude toward the possibility of human goodness. If Swift attacked human nature as depraved, he was simply being orthodox. From the point of view of many modern scholars, the author of the *Essays* contradicts himself, for part of the second charge disproves the first.

In the 1920's Swift criticism and scholarship began to make a not

[14] Louis Landa, "Jonathan Swift and Charity," *JEGP,* XLIV (October, 1945), 338.

[15] In reviewing Middleton Murry's biography, Irvin Ehrenpreis speaks of "Swift's profoundly orthodox piety," *PQ,* XXXIV (July, 1955), 323.

[16] See also, for example, this same pattern in Quintana's *Mind and Art,* pp. 67–70; Max Korn, *Die Weltanschauung Jonathan Swifts* (Jena: Biedermann, 1935), pp. 44, 60; C. J. Horne, "Introduction," *Swift on His Age* (London: G. Harrap, 1953), pp. 15, 47; Irvin Ehrenpreis, *The Personality of Jonathan Swift* (London: Methuen, 1958), pp. 67–70.

[17] B. A. Goldgar, *The Curse of Party* (Lincoln: University of Nebraska Press, 1961), p. 23. No citations to Swift's works are given as proof for this assertion.

[18] *Ibid.,* p. 49.

always good use of a new discipline, the history of ideas. By reflecting
on the developments of thought in the Renaissance and in the seventeenth century, and by searching the pages of Swift for parallels to the
attitudes and ideas of the sceptical-Christian tradition, T. O. Wedel
was able to identify Swift with that tradition.[19] And, today, to say that
a poet or satirist was "in one of the great traditions of the West" is a
kind of praise. Since Wedel, critics have examined the writings of Justus
Lipsius and others in the Senecan and neo-Stoic tradition, and discovered that Swift is a neo-Stoic;[20] have read the sceptical humanists
and Catholics like Montaigne and Pascal, and discovered that Swift is
the opposite of a neo-Stoic—that is, a Christian sceptic;[21] have studied
the ideas of Hobbes and Gassendi, representative of Renaissance neo-
Epicureanism, and discovered that Swift is opposed to materialism and
atheism;[22] or have read the British empiricists and nominalists, and
found that Swift belongs in their camp.[23] Such a method tends to become a consideration of a (preselected) tradition and those elements in
Swift's writings which are in, or can be forced into, agreement (or
disagreement) with that tradition. In nearly every case, in the interest
of constructing a "coherent" explanation of Swift's thought, the complexity of his thinking is ignored.

Some acute scholars in eighteenth-century studies have begun to
explore the "Augustan middle way" in ethics, as it applies to Pope and
Swift. This scholarship gets its impetus from Lovejoy's summary of the
consequences of the principle of plenitude in ethics and politics:

> In the earlier part of the [18th] century, the most significant of these
> [consequences], and the most characteristic, may be described as a coun-
> sel of imperfection—an ethics of prudent mediocrity. The method of
> such an ethics would consist in taking stock of man's actual constitution
> —his distinguishing instincts, desires, and natural capacities—and in
> formulating his good in terms of some balances and practicable ful-
> fillment of these. And since man's place is not a very high one, since he
> is a mixture of the animal and the intellectual elements, and since the
> latter is present in him only in a meagre measure and in its lowest, or
> almost lowest, form, the beginning of wisdom for him was to remember
> and to hold fast to his limitations.

Lovejoy further points out that such ethics:

[19] Wedel, "Philosophical Background," *SP*.
[20] Quintana, *Mind and Art*, pp. 59 ff.
[21] Wedel himself does this, as does Ehrenpreis, *The Personality of Jonathan Swift*,
pp. 91, 99, 109, 114.
[22] Miriam Starkman, *Swift's Satire on Learning in "A Tale of a Tub"* (Princeton:
Princeton University Press, 1950), pp. 23 ff.
[23] This is the argument of an unpublished dissertation (Columbia University,
1954) by James McNelis, "The Education of Lemuel Gulliver."

. . . also . . . led to a disparagement of all the more pretentious and exacting moral ideals—for example, of that of Stoicism. A creature so limited and so near to the other animals in kind if not in kinship, must necessarily be incapable of attaining any very high level of political wisdom or virtue, and that consequently no great improvement in men's behavior or in the organization of society could be hoped for.[24]

Lovejoy illustrates his points with lines from Pope, and Maynard Mack has shown (with careful attention to the complexities involved) that "by taking account of [man's] limitations," Pope sought to "discover [man's] potentialities."[25] The natural consequence of the discovery of Pope's place in an ideational low-pressure system has been the conclusion that Swift, too, lowered the moral demands on human nature:

> . . . the extraordinary views of Gulliver's Houyhnhnmland have been repeatedly cited as identical with Swift's. And this despite the fact that the incidents of the book show the author to be studiedly undercutting his hero-gull and to be using the metaphor of the rational *animal*, the Houyhnhnm, to make it plain that pure rationality is neither available nor appropriate to the human species—just as in the "Essay on Man" Pope's fully rational angels show "a Newton as we show an Ape."[26]

Thus the way was cleared for Kathleen Williams to discover that Swift was really a historically premature, sensitively tolerant post-Freudian: ". . . he believed in tolerance, compassion, responsiveness to one another's individual needs."[27] Miss Williams is not speaking of someone like William Faulkner or Middleton Murry, as one might suspect, but of Jonathan Swift.

If Swift did expect little from man because man is capable of little (besides tolerance, compassion, and the like), then one is faced with a host of puzzles, which cannot be worked by attributing them to Swift's ironic technique. First, Swift had the habit of speaking of virtue as if it were not only the most important thing, but as if it also actually exists;[28] and he continually speaks of an animal that he calls "a wise and good man."[29] And even though the Scots were, to Swift, a species lower on the chain of being than homo sapiens, he could speak about one Scot, the Marquess of Montrose, in the following terms:

[24] Arthur O. Lovejoy, *The Great Chain of Being* (New York: Harper, 1960, paperback), pp. 200–203.
[25] Maynard Mack, "Introduction" to the Twickenham edition of *An Essay on Man* (New Haven: Yale University Press, 1950), p. lxix.
[26] Maynard Mack, "The Muse of Satire," *Yale Review*, XLI (Autumn, 1951), 84.
[27] K. Williams, *Swift and the Age of Compromise*, p. 216. Fulton Catlin has been able to reach much the same conclusion in "Swift's Moral Realism in *Gulliver's Travels*," *Summary of Doctoral Dissertations*, University of Wisconsin, XIII (1953), 378.
[28] C, IV, 77, 204; V, 17, 85, 150, 171; PW, VI, 176; VII, 30.
[29] PW, II, 1, 24; VIII, 45, 85; XII, 102; XIII, 74; TS, XI, 179.

The onely Honest Scot. He was the onely Man in Scotland who had
ever one Grain of Virtue; and was therefore abhorred and murdered
publickly by his hellish Countrymen. A perfect Hero, wholly un-Scotified.
(PW, V, 310, 316, 317).

And in the feigned autobiographical account of "The Last Speech and
Dying Words of Ebenezor Elliston" that famous underworld character
states that even he knows one honest man, with whom he leaves a list of
his confederates in crime, which list is to be given to the authorities if
his friends do not give up their robbing and killing (PW, IX, 39).
Evidently the criminals believed, with "Ebenezor," that one honest
man was alive in Dublin, if we can accept Sir Walter Scott's statement
that there was a great decrease in the crime rate in Dublin for some
time thereafter.[30]

But there is better proof that Swift did not take a complacent view of
human nature, nor lower the goals—ideals they are often called, for
what reason I cannot imagine; good sense and good nature are basic
facts in every man's experience, although rare; it is just as sensible to
speak of measles as an ideal disease, because every one does not have it.
In the *Intelligencer* Swift studied the careers of two imaginary clergymen in order to discover why it is that men of "discretion" get on so
well, especially in the Church. It is best to consider first the second
career, that of Eugenio, the gifted one, who had some talent for poetry,
whose "chief Study was the Authors of Antiquity," and who was learned
in Greek and Latin:

He was a thousand Times recommended by his poetical Friends to great
Persons, as a young Man of excellent Parts, who deserved Encourage-
ment; and received a thousand Promises: But his Modesty, and a generous Spirit, which disdained the Slavery of continual Application and
Attendance, always disappointed him; making room for vigilant Dunces,
who were sure to be never out of Sight. . . . He had an excellent Faculty
in preaching, if he were not sometimes a little too refined, and apt to
trust too much in his own Way of thinking and reasoning. (PW, XII,
45)

This superior man, a man of virtue by Swift's account, spends nearly
the whole of his life in a remote vicarage.

Corusodes (his name suggests sniveling namby-pambyism), however,
a dullard and an enemy to wit, lets his principles follow his economic
interests, lends money at ten per cent, keeps a bad house, and treats
"all his Inferiors of the Clergy with a most sanctified Pride." He advances rapidly, "without the Merit of one single Virtue; moderately

[30] Scott, p. 263.

stocked with the least valuable Parts of Erudition: utterly devoid of all Taste, Judgment, or Genius; and in his Grandeur naturally chusing to hawl up others after him, whose Accomplishments most resemble his own." In this ascent to greatness, a most valuable trait was a ready acceptance of the limits of human nature (such as Swift is accused of having, by the author of the 1714 *Essays* and by modern scholars):

> Power, in whatever Hands, or whatever Party, was always secure of his most charitable Opinion. He had many wholsome Maxims ready to excuse all Miscarriages of State: Men are but Men; *Erunt vitia donec homines;* and *Quod supra nos, nihil ad nos:* With several others of equal weight. (PW, XII, 41–45)

Can Swiftian apologists attribute to Swift the very opinions that he gave to Corusodes, the church-climber without taste, wit, learning, or virtue? Indeed Swift condemns such maxims as *unwholesome* by calling them Corusodes'. "Men are but men," "there will be vices as long as there are men," and "what is above us is not exacted of us"—all are complacent sentiments which found no place in Swift's lacerated heart.

In the history of Swift criticism, along with the views begun by the 1714 *Essays,* has existed a countertheme, more subdued and often ignored, that in Swift's satires "all qualities . . . inherently praiseworthy [e.g., "self-sacrifice, courage, simple good sense"] do not appear invalidated at all."[31] Even the early biographers, who can be cited as in agreement with the Benevolists,[32] were aware that there was a side of Swift besides that which his enemies called cynicism. Orrery discovered, for example, that Swift's poetry, despite occasional vulgarity and denigration of human nature, "always contained some secret marks of wisdom, and deep morality," and that "throughout his various correspondence you will discover very strong marks of an anxious, benevolent friend: And, to my great pleasure, I find the misanthrope often lost in the good-natured man."[33] And Delany found that Swift was highly sensitive to human goodness: "Swift loved merit wherever he found it, and never seemed more delighted, than when he could draw it out from obscurity, into an advantageous light, and exalt it there."[34]

Perhaps we are so little aware of this side of Swift's mind because the only book which makes that its major theme is a long, repetitious, and (according to Dr. Johnson) unnaturally dull book, the biography by

[31] G. Wilson Knight, *The Burning Oracle* (London: Oxford University Press, 1939), p. 118.
[32] Orrery, p. 41; Delany, p. 170.
[33] Orrery, pp. 80, 161.
[34] Delany, pp. 27, 226. See also Deane Swift, p. 227 (Actually 226, but misnumbered).

Thomas Sheridan. When Sheridan says that Swift is a moralist he apparently intends something more than modern critics do when using the same term: ". . . all his life a votary to virtue," Swift was exact "in the practice of the higher virtues [justice, temperance, and fortitude] even with a stoical severity; and none of the great characters of antiquity, were, on that account, more entitled to our esteem and admiration." Sheridan also seems to think that Swift the moralist was aware of the fact that there are worthy as well as unworthy men in this world, the virtuous few who alone deserve admiration and respect:

> [Swift] was the first man of letters and genius that we read of, who asserted the superiority of talents over titles, of virtue over wealth, in the face of the great and the rich; and not content with vain speculations, and idly declaiming on the subject, as all others had done, boldly demanded and received, the homage due to such superiority, both for himself and others.[35]

Some few modern critics, like G. Wilson Knight and Middleton Murry, agree with these statements by the early biographers.[36] And others see in Swift the disillusioned idealist, who sincerely prefers good qualities in man but finds them wanting or rare.[37] The most valuable insights, however, are those of the nineteenth century. With succinctness, Leslie Stephen summarizes Swift's basic belief: "His doctrine was, briefly, that: virtue was the only thing which deserved love and admiration; and yet that virtue in this hideous chaos of a world, involved misery and decay."[38] Hazlitt makes his point with great art:

> [Swift] has taken a new view of human nature, such as a being of a higher sphere might take of it; he has torn the scales from off his moral vision; he has tried an experiment upon human life, and sifted its pretensions from the alloy of circumstances; he has measured it with a rule, has weighed it in a balance, and found it, for the most part, wanting and worthless—in substance and in shew. Nothing solid, nothing

[35] Sheridan, pp. 121, 298, 420.

[36] Knight, *The Burning Oracle*, pp. 114–130; Middleton Murry, *Jonathan Swift* (London: J. Cape, 1954), pp. 33, 51–52, 339, 484.

[37] In the following the point is made that Swift was a true satirist, as described by Louis Bredvold: ". . . in the true satirist, derision is limited and tempered by moral idealism," "A Note in Defense of Satire," *ELH*, VII (December, 1940), 264: A. E. Case, *Four Essays on "Gulliver's Travels"* (Princeton: Princeton University Press, 1945), pp. 110, 111, 123, Read, *The Sense of Glory*, p. 88, George Sherburn, "Errors concerning the Houyhnhnms," *MP*, LVI (November, 1958), 92–97, J. C. Squire, "The Utopian Satirist," *Life and Letters* (New York: George H. Doran, 1921), pp. 137–144, F. M. Darnall, "Old Wine in New Bottles," *South Atlantic Quarterly*, XLI (January, 1942), 53–63, W. B. C. Watkins, *Perilous Balance* (Princeton: Princeton University Press, 1935), pp. 1–4, Charles Whibley, *Literary Studies* (London: Macmillan, 1919), pp. 343–370.

[38] Leslie Stephen, *Swift* (London: Macmillan, 1931), pp. 49–50.

valuable is left in his system but virtue and wisdom. What a libel is this upon mankind! What a convincing proof of misanthropy! What presumption of *malice prepense,* to shew men what they are, and to teach them what they ought to be! . . . I cannot see the harm, the misanthropy, the immoral and degrading tendency of this. The moral lesson is as fine as the intellectual exhibition is amusing. It is an attempt to tear off the mask of imposture from the world; and nothing but imposture has a right to complain of it. It is, indeed, the way with our quacks in morality to preach up the dignity of human nature, to pamper pride and hypocrisy with the idle mockeries of the virtues they pretend to, and which they have not: but it was not Swift's way to cant morality or any thing else; nor did his genius prompt him to write unmeaning panegyrics on mankind![39]

Nothing is left, nothing but wisdom and virtue.

II

Benevolent Anti-Benevolist

Swift's sermons have afforded scholars occasion and evidence, in recent years, for showing his attitude toward the Deists and the ancient moralists.[40] The effort of such scholarship has been to put Swift in a conservative Anglican position with regard to morals. But the sermons are also a source of evidence of Swift's independence of mind (like Eugenio's). For Swift, virtue was unselfish benevolent action. In a sermon he prays for restoration of the "great Duty of Brotherly Love or Charity among us, the very Bond of Peace, and of all Virtues" (PW, IX, 179); and he asks, in another sermon, "What is there, that can give a generous Spirit more Pleasure and Complacency of Mind, than to consider, that he is an Instrument of doing much Good?" (PW, IX, 148). In his correspondence he speaks of the same generous spirit, in a self-depreciating way:

I hear they think me a smart Dean; and that I am for doing good. My notion is, that if a man cannot mend the public he should mend old shoes if he can do no better; and therefore I endeavour in the little sphere I am placed to do all the good it is capable of. (C, ii, 265; cf. C, II, 293)

---

[39] William Hazlitt, "Lecture VI," *Lectures on the English Poets.* I quote from *The Complete Works of William Hazlitt,* ed. P. P. Howe, V (London: J. M. Dent, 1930), 110–111.

[40] K. Williams, *Swift and the Age of Compromise,* pp. v, 154 ff.; Louis Landa, "Swift, the Mysteries, and Deism," *UTSE* (1944), pp. 239–256. Landa, however, who probably inadvertently suggested to critics that Swift's dislike of Deism be applied to explicate *Gulliver's Travels,* has disagreed with such criticism—see his review of Ehrenpreis's *Personality of Jonathan Swift, PQ,* XXXVIII (July, 1959), 352.

Swift finds the only advantage of the rich over the poor in their "Power of doing Good to others" (PW, IX, 194); and he says that all the blessings of life are to be used for benevolent purposes, "doing Acts of Charity and Generosity": "to protect the Innocent, to relieve the Oppressed, and to punish the Oppressor"; "to instruct the Ignorant, to be a faithful Counsellor either in publick or private, to be a Director of Youth" (PW, IX, 148–149).

But Swift's thinking in this matter does not follow completely the opinion of the Anglican Benevolists, or of the philosopher-Benevolists. His concept of benevolence takes a Roman[41] or Machiavellian form. For Swift, benevolent action is public action not, broadly, action for the good of mankind or one's neighbor. Consider the unconventional interpretation that Swift gives to the commandment "love thy neighbor":

> Nature directs every one of us, and God permits us, to consult our own private Good before the private Good of any other person whatsoever. We are, indeed, commanded to love our Neighbour as ourselves, but not as well as ourselves. . . . the law of nature, which is the law of God, obligeth me to take care of myself first, and afterwards of him. . . . beside this love we owe to every man in his particular capacity under the title of our neighbour, there is yet a duty of a more large, extensive nature, incumbent on us; which is, our love to our neighbour in his public capacity, as he is a member of that great body, the commonwealth, under the same government with ourselves; and this is usually called *love of the public,* and is *a duty to which we are more strictly obliged than even that of loving ourselves;* because therein ourselves are also contained, as well as all our neighbours, in one great body. This love of the public, or of the commonwealth, or love of our country, was in antient times *properly* known by the name of Virtue, *because it was the greatest of all virtues,* and was supposed to contain all virtues in it: And many great examples of this virtue are left us on record, scarcely to be believed, or even conceived, in such a base, corrupted, wicked age as this we live in. In those times it was common for men to sacrifice their lives for the good of their country, although they had neither hope or belief of future rewards; whereas, in our days, very few make the least scruple of sacrificing a whole nation, as well as their own souls, for a little present gain; which often hath been known to end in their own ruin in this world, as it certainly must in that to come. (PW, IX, 232–233; italics mine)

Contrast this with the notion of benevolence which R. S. Crane has found in scores of Anglican sermons before and during Swift's time:

[41] Roman virtue is discussed in Chapter 4. Swift seems to have been aware that love of the public or of one's country is a pagan virtue: "However, I am sorry that, although Christianity be much out of fashion, there might not be some remainder of pagan virtues, such as justice, and honour, and learning, and love of our country left," C, VI, 12–13.

that virtue is "universal benevolence."[42] Swift also implies that love of one's country is a natural affection: "All offences against our country have this aggravation, that they are ungrateful and unnatural" (PW, IX, 239):

> ... we are obliged [by God] to act, as far as our Power reacheth, towards the Good of the whole Community. And he who doth not perform that Part assigned him towards advancing the Benefit of the Whole, in proportion to his Opportunities and Abilities, is not only a useless, but a very mischievous Member of the Publick: Because he taketh his Share of the Profit, and yet leaveth his Share of the Burden to be borne by others, which is the true principal Cause of most Miseries and Misfortunes in Life. For, a wise Man who doth not assist with his Counsels, a great Man with his Protection, a rich Man with his Bounty and Charity, and a poor Man with his Labour, are perfect Nusances in a Commonwealth. (PW, IX, 142)

This point will bear stressing, since it is usually overlooked and since it shows Swift out of agreement with an increasingly popular Church opinion *and with the Deists,* who found personal friendship and the more cosmopolitian notion of universal benevolence to be virtues. Bolingbroke, for example, vigorously disagreed with what Swift advanced "with the air of a maxim, that exile is the greatest punishment of men of virtue, because virtue consists in loving our country" (C, III, 210). But that is a maxim which Swift continually advanced.[43]

A little anecdote told by Delany beautifully illustrates Swift's opinion and shows how he disagreed with one Benevolist:

> I have also, heard him say, that one evening, the conversation [between Swift and Addison] happened to turn upon the most distinguished characters in the history of the old testament: in which, Swift preferred and supported, that of Joseph; and Addison, that of Jonathan: and after they had urged their reasons on both sides, with a good deal of zeal, for a considerable time; Mr. Addison smiled, and said, he was glad no third person was witness to their dispute: recollecting at once that he was asserting the hero of Swift's name, and Swift the hero of his: which might be interpreted by a third person, as an intended compliment, of each, to the other. Whereas, in truth, nothing was more undesigned, or remote from their thoughts.[44]

---

[42] R. S. Crane, "Suggestions toward a Genealogy of the Man of Feeling," *ELH*, I (November, 1934), 205–230. "Charity was one of their favorite themes: not the charity which was primarily love of God; not charity merely to the parish poor or to fellow Christians, but a 'general kindness' to all men because they are men, an active desire to relieve their sufferings, if not to alter the social conditions in which they live; the kind of charity best described by the words—more common in the eighteenth century, but already coming into use [in the late seventeenth]—'humanity,' 'good nature,' 'universal benevolence' " (p. 211).

[43] See, e.g., PW, X, 69, 71, 83, 91; XII, 55; XIII, 79–88.

[44] Delany, p. 33.

It is Joseph the provider, the incorruptible, the man of great public wisdom, that Swift admires, not Jonathan, and the self-denial, self-sacrifice, and bravery in his friendship for David.

This is not to deny that Swift valued good nature and friendship highly. He praises good nature and seems to regard it at times as an accidental natural endowment[45]—we would say, a matter of the glands —and at times as the product of education and religion. I would judge that the principle involved here constitutes the really significant reason for his preference of Christian ethics over pagan, insofar as he makes that preference: "The Christian doctrine teacheth us all those dispositions that make us affable and courteous, gentle, and kind, without any morose leaven of pride or vanity, which entered into the composition of most Heathen schemes" (PW, IX, 248).

If we believe the author of the 1714 *Essays,* Swift thought that all friendship was feigned or imaginary; and Swift's two poems on his own death lend credence to this view, with their theme derived from a maxim of La Rochefoucauld: "In the Adversity of our best Friends, we find something that doth not displease us" (P, II, 551). But in those poems Swift speaks of himself, and scandal undeserved is praise in disguise; his correspondence with Pope, Gay, Arbuthnot, Bolingbroke, and Pulteney disproves the assertions in the poetry (P, II, 555). At times Swift could give Bolingbrokesque, Epicurean advice: to ignore the world and cultivate private friendship (C, III, 267; V, 1).

In truth, Swift seems almost to have been too sanguine about the possibility of friendship, especially of others toward himself. He would hardly appear so disillusioned if he had not trusted too much in the goodness of his own motives as well as those of others. His entire career might well be interpreted from this point of view. Because he trusted too much in the friendship, good will, and justice of Temple, King William, Lord Somers, the Irish bishops, Queen Anne, Princess (later Queen) Caroline—exactly because of this trust was he disturbed at not getting what he had reason to expect: appointments for himself and for the men whom he recommended, and relief for the Irish. The most telling proof of this interpretation may be Swift's almost filial trust in Harley's friendship, even though (as Swift must not have known) Harley neglected Swift's claims, in the years 1711 to 1714, in order to aggrandize his own family. C. H. Firth has published a careful study of the appointments that Harley was responsible for.[46] This study ends in a

[45] See his remarks on Cato and Socrates in Chapter 4.
[46] C. H. Firth, "Dean Swift and Ecclesiastical Preferment," *RES,* II (January, 1926), 1–17.

significant way; after surveying the evidence, which shows that Harley engaged in something like jobbery to improve the status of his family, while ignoring Swift's claims for appointment, Firth quotes a letter from Swift to Harley's son, in which Swift asks to have the use of any papers that Harley left, in order to include whatever they contain in a biography he intends to write: ". . . such a work most properly belongs to me, who loved and respected him [Harley] above all men, and had the honour to know him better than any other of my level did" (C, III, 197). The happier question for a historian to pose is whether Harley ever had reason to complain of Swift's trustworthiness.

Swift was at first deluded about the friendship between Harley and St. John; perhaps he fell into such an error because his pet notion was that of the communion of men of genius:

> I have often endeavoured to establish a friendship among all men of genius, and would fain have it done. They are seldom above three or four contemporaries, and if they could be united, would drive the world before them. (C, III, 175)

He wrote to Peterborough, in 1711:

> I have told them [Harley and St. John] more than once, upon occasion, that all my hopes of their success depended on their union, that I saw they loved one another, and hoped they would continue it, to remove the scandal of inconstancy ascribed to Court friendships. I am not now so secure. (C, I, 253)

In the same letter he flattered Peterborough by suggesting that his virtue suited him for living at the height of the Roman republic, rather than in England in the eighteenth century; Swift got a disillusioning reply: "You were returning me to ages past. . . . I find matter in yours to send you as far back as the golden age. How came you to frame a system—in the times we live in—to govern the world by love?" (C, I, 262).[47] Swift's interpretation of his friendship with Stella and Vanessa was surely "idealistic" (P, II, 711, 725); and his "worst" opinion was not cynical: love for others may not ultimately be egoistic, but the extent of one's true friendship is limited, as Swift explained to Pope: "Your notions of friendship are new to me; I believe every man is born with his *quantum*, and he cannot give to one without robbing another" (C, III, 175).

There seems to have been widespread agreement in Swift's day that the important virtues were the social ones, agreeing among the Benevolists and the Utilitarians, among men like Berkeley, Bolingbroke, Pope,

---

[47] See PW, VIII, 87–88, 144.

and Locke.[48] Hobbes himself belongs in the same company, for he also thought that the virtues are precisely the benevolent traits in mankind. For Hobbes, the state of nature is a state of way of every man against every man:

> [In this] condition of mere nature, which is a condition of war . . . private appetite is the measure of good and evil: and consequently all men agree on this, that peace is good, and therefore also the way, or means of peace, which, as I have shewed before, are justice, gratitude, modesty, equity, mercy, and the rest of the laws of nature, are good; that is to say, moral virtues; and their contrary vices, evil. . . . the writers of moral philosophy [prior to Hobbes did not see] wherein consisted the goodness [of the virtues—namely in their being] the means of peaceable, sociable, and comfortable living.[49]

Recalling Swift's attitude toward pride[50] and his reasons for preferring Christian to pagan ethics, we can tentatively place him in a general movement of thought, which Leo Strauss interprets as greatly influenced by Hobbes:

> If virtue is identified with peaceableness, vice will become identical with that habit or that passion which is per se incompatible with peace because it essentially and, as it were, of set purpose issues in offending others; vice becomes identical for all practical purposes with pride or vanity or *amour-propre* rather than with dissoluteness or weakness of the soul. In other words, if virtue is reduced to social virtue or to benevolence or kindness or "the liberal virtues," "the severe virtues" of self-restraint will lose their standing.[51]

III

JUSTICE

The classical teaching was that justice is getting what one deserves, or rewards according to deserts. This teaching was implicit in the original meaning of the term *aristocracy,* the rule of the best: in strict justice, only the best have the right, only the best deserve, to rule. Although he rejects this doctrine, Hume explains it very well:

> We shall suppose that a creature possessed of reason, but unacquainted with human nature, deliberates with himself what rules of justice or property would best promote public interest and establish peace and

---

[48] For Locke's views, see *Some Thoughts concerning Education* in *The Works of John Locke,* 10th ed. (London: Bye & Law, 1801), IX, Nos. 67, 104, 105, 110, 116, 117.

[49] *Leviathan,* XII, XV (82, 104).

[50] See Chapter 2.

[51] Leo Strauss, *Natural Right and History* (Chicago: University of Chicago Press, 1953), p. 188.

security among mankind: his most obvious thought would be to assign the largest possessions to the most extensive virtue and give everyone the power of doing good, proportioned to his inclination.[52]

Swift, I fear, is such an imaginative, rational creature, for that is his principle of justice exactly, although not one which he felt ever likely to prevail generally in a society. It was the governing principle in most of his action, whether in selecting friends (C, III, 118) or in seeking preferment for his friends or strangers. The dominant principle in his treatment of others, it is perhaps what gives us an impression of tension in his thoughts—between his political opinions, on the one hand, that seem to assume that man is a dangerous, egoistic animal, which must be forced into peaceableness (see Chapter 5), and, on the other, his passionate devotion to the principle of the right of merit to honor and authority.

Such a view of justice entails the belief in the existence of virtue, or the distinction between men of virtue and ordinary men, as can be easily seen in the story of Corusodes and Eugenio, discussed above. Swift's understanding of human nature is never properly known if this distinction, which he constantly employed, is ignored. Delany and Sheridan emphatically attest, as do his letters, to the extreme "partiality" of Swift toward men of merit, and to his energy and perception in detecting merit.[53] Swift seems to have been exceptionally good at finding and befriending the worthiest of his age; and that is the explanation of his motto: *cum magnis vixisse*.[54]

One of the Whigs that Swift admired was Lord Carteret, Lieutenant of Ireland during the turmoil over Wood's Halfpence. In a little poetic tribute to him, "The Birth of Manly Virtue," Swift gives direct expression to his principle of justice: "True Virtue has a Right to rise" (P, II, 386). And Swift was not blind to the same element in Addison's career: ". . . it is a prodigious singularity in any Court to owe one's rise entirely to merit" (C, II, 395).

Swift's own merit, his justice, claims our attention in his many efforts on behalf of those whom he felt were deserving, and nowhere more greatly to his honor than in the case of George Berkeley, a case where no one can deny either Swift's great assistance or the beneficiary's great merit. Swift wrote in the *Journal to Stella*, "I am bound to in honor & Conscience, to use all my little Credit towards helping forward Men of

[52] *Inquiry concerning the Principles of Morals* (New York: Liberal Arts Press, 1957), Section III, Part II, No. 2, pp. 23–24.
[53] Delany, p. 27; Sheridan, p. 121.
[54] Delany, p. 267; see also Orrery, p. 42.

Worth in the world" (J, II, 659).[55] Neither the strength of this conviction nor the number of men benefitted from it can be overestimated.[56]

The purpose of the Brothers Club, or The Society, as explained by Swift, involves three of his dearest principles: "The end of our Club is to advance [1] conversation and [2] friendship, and [3] to reward deserving persons with our interest and recommendation" (J, I, 294). Swift prided himself on being a just, or an "honest judicious recommender" (C, V, 170). And he refused to accept any recommendation other than talent or virtue, as can be seen in the humorous justice with which Swift directed a bit of business indifferent to him, although important to the Church: the appointment of singers to the choir at St. Patrick's. Swift's friends, who wrote to use a little influence in a minor matter, got unequivocal replies:

> You are to understand that in disposing these musical employments, I determine to act directly contrary to Ministers of State, by giving them to those who best deserve. (C, III, 46)

> If we want a singer, and I can get a better [than the man you recommend], that better shall be preferred, although my father were competitor. (C, II, 72)

That last flourish is not mere rhetoric; Swift rarely used his influence for his relatives, who he said had "not a grain of merit among them" (C, V, 170; cf. C, IV, 144). Therefore, he leaves them unpreferred, acting on his "own speculative motions of virtue" (C, V, 172)—or, as he also explains it, being "void of what the world calls natural affection" for his relatives, whom he believed to be "degenerating from their ancestors" (C, VI, 126). Such a principle of justice is as inflexible, impersonal, rigorous, and severe as that espoused by the strictest of the ancient moralists '—or those cold, rational animals, the Houyhnhnms'.[57]

Swift did not, of course, hope for much justice in actual political regimes, but on one occasion he appeared as a most sanguine projector, who issued to the Queen, in *A Project for the Advancement of Religion and Morals,* this audacious injunction: be just!—delegate power to and confer honor only on those who "cultivate Religion and Virtue." And he pointed out the other side of the coin. Just reward encourages virtue: ". . . it is in the Power of the Prince to make Piety and Virtue become

[55] See C, III, 212–213, 262.
[56] See PW, III, 12, 98–99; C, III, 248–249; V, 17.
[57] From a Christian point of vantage, C. S. Lewis calls such a view "ruthless," *English Literature in the Sixteenth Century* (Oxford: Clarendon Press, 1954), p. 10.

the Fashion of the Age; if at the same Time he would make them neces-sary Qualifications for Favour and Preferment" (PW, II, 47).

Finally, it is in the name of justice that Swift prefers Christian moral theory to any other, and in particular finds pagan ethics sometimes in-adequate, as when it leaves "the wise and the good man wholly at the mercy of uncertain chance" (PW, IX, 246). Virtue needing some en-dowment, human nature being so "constituted, that we can never pur-sue any thing heartily but upon hopes of a reward" (PW, IX, 244), it is necessary that Providence exist, to reward virtue, to do it justice, in the afterlife, and to encourage it in his life. "It rarely happens that Men are rewarded by the Publick for their Justice and Virtue; neither do those who act upon such Principles, expect any Recompence until the next World" (PW, III, 137).[58]

IV

USEFULNESS AND AMIABILITY

Much of what Swift thought to be virtue can be deduced from his comments on vice, as he explains in his sermon "False Witness": "In describing to you the several Kinds of false Witnesses, I have made it less necessary to dwell much longer upon this Head [the virtue of faith-ful witnessing]; because a faithful Witness, like every Thing else, is known by his contrary" (PW, IX, 188). To judge by their contraries (discussed in Chapter 2), the following are virtues: humility, humanity, kindness, liberality, mercy, candor, sincerity, good will, sympathy, and justice—to consider only the social virtues. We get an interesting indi-cation of the importance of these virtues in Swift's praise of Arbuthnot: ". . . our Doctor has every quality and virtue that can make a man *amiable* or *useful*" (C, III, 278; italics mine).

It is necessary to round out a discussion of Swift's views on human nature by listing at least a few of the lesser qualities and virtues which he discovered and praised in man. As the comment on Arbuthnot sug-

[58] Interestingly enough, like modern liberals, Hobbes thought such a view of justice as here described to be wrong. He puts the ruler in the same position as God, who lets the sun shine on the just and unjust alike. As Hobbes says, ". . . merit . . . is not due by justice; but is rewarded of grace only," *Leviathan*, XV (98). For Hobbes, justice is keeping one's contracts, the second law of nature. Of course the primary contract is the one which created society, which means that men contract in such a way as to create injustice (from Swift's point of view). In Part IV of *Gulliver's Travels* is brilliant satiric cut at Hobbes' theory that by consent men give up, when they enter society, whatever claims they have by nature. The Houyhnhnm Master says to Gulliver: "Nature hath left you utterly uncapable of doing much Mischief: For your Mouths lying flat with your Faces, you can hardly bite each other to any Purpose, unless by Consent" (IV, v, 6).

gests, many virtues praised by Swift entail a utility principle, although he does not analyze the virtues to find a common principle. The general drift of his praise is in the direction of those traits which make social intercourse more pleasing:

Humility, modesty   (P, I, 33 ff.; J, I, 275; PW, II, 187; PW, III, 99).
Wit   (C, III, 207).
Decency   (P, II, 593).
Good manners   (TS, XI, 79–88).
Pleasant, sensible conversation   (C, V, 1; PW, IV, 87 ff.).
Loyalty, gratitude   (PW, III, 19; PW, VI, 183).
Candor, sincerity   (C, III, 271).
Cleanliness   (C, I, 35; C, V, 269–270).

V

PERSONAL WORTH

Some virtues—for example, wisdom, and learning—deserve praise on the grounds of their social usefulness as well as their contribution to personal excellence. Swift seems to have valued highly the piety of Arbuthnot, as simply the epitome of Christian excellence; and he pays the highest tribute to Arbuthnot and William Sancroft (C, V, 107; P, I, 33 ff.). Piety, however, or ostensible piety, is a socially beneficial trait, even if it involves hypocrisy. Consider the way that Swift speaks of Orrery's piety: ". . . you believe a God and Providence; . . . you are a firm Christian, according to the doctrine of the Church established in both kingdoms [England and Ireland]" (C, V, 28). He almost makes conformity a virtue: ". . . in a country already Christian, to bring so fundamental a point of faith [as Christ's divinity] into debate, can have no consequences that are not pernicious to morals and public peace" (PW, IX, 262). Swift also could say, facetiously, "I believe, it is often with Religion as it is with Love; which, by much Dissembling, at last grows real" (PW, II, 57).

Swift's admiration of genius and learning and the many instances of his paying homage and giving assistance to those possessing either are well known,[59] as is his limited respect for philosophy and "intellectualism" not immediately concerned with common social life or morals.[60] One might say that he valued wisdom, but not philosophy, at least as it was practised in his day and in medieval and modern universities. Probably, I would suggest, Swift's aversion to the "purer" activities of the intellect and to the intricacies of dialectic developed out of his ad-

[59] PW, IV, 19; C, I, 366; III, 271; V, 150.
[60] See Quintana, *Mind and Art*, pp. 55–59.

herence (like most in his age) to the principle capsulized in Pope's line, "The proper study of Mankind is Man," out of his agreement with a bias of his age which has been called "anti-intellectualism,"[61] and out of his physiology and health. He was a most active man by nature, hardly given to habits sufficiently sedentary for intense speculation. Also, his bad health drove him to seek relief in exercise and travel (cf. C, V, 19).[62] Wisdom, in the sense that is implied in the root meaning *philosophy* (love of wisdom), is not for Swift the final excellence of human nature, although in one place he speaks of wisdom and genius as inducing, if not infallibly producing, good morals (C, V, 150). Brutus and Cato, learned and scholarly patriots and gentlemen, are his heroes, not the philosopher-statesman Cicero (C, III, 110; see Chapter 4).[63]

The sterner virtues, chastity and temperance, as noted in Chapter 2, seldom engaged Swift's attention. But there is some ambiguity in Swift's understanding of temperance. He admired Socrates and Cato as great models of temperance and fortitude (PW, IX, 249); and he seems to have understood temperance in the classical sense, as a tempering of the body so that there is a harmony between appetites and principles. He wrote to Pope: ". . . is not temperance a necessary virtue for great men, since it is the parent of ease and liberty, so necessary for the use and improvement of the mind, and which philosophy allows to be the greatest felicities of life?" (C, IV, 35). According to the ancients, the temperate man was thus freed from the struggles of desire, freed to participate in higher things—virtue and wisdom.

Swift admonished Charles Ford, who was prone to eat and drink too much, to be temperate, but not in the ancient sense. "I do not mean in point of morality but health."[64] It is easy to see in the famous paradox of Mandeville's—private vices, public virtues—how the new utilitarian ethics was weakening the older view of temperance; and the same kind of thinking is still represented today in the form of the belief that prosperity (public happiness) depends on competition, which depends on incentive, which is exactly intemperate desire. Besides that, if amiability

[61] Arthur O. Lovejoy, "The Parallel of Deism and Classicism," *Essays in the History of Ideas* (New York: Putnam, 1960), p. 89. First printed in *MP*, XXIX (February, 1932), 281–299.

[62] Gulliver speaks of himself at the beginning of Book II as "condemned by Nature and Fortune to an active and restless Life."

[63] Swift had greater respect for Roman statesmen than for Greek philosophers. Cicero himself, while more the philosopher than Brutus or Cato, was inclined to value the social virtue, justice, more than the philosophic one, wisdom. See *De Officiis*, II, ix–x.

[64] LF, 136; cf. 132, 160. Swift implies temperance is not a virtue: ". . . many a moral and pious man's health is ruined by intemperance," LF, 145.

is valued highly intemperance cannot be too vicious, since many amiable men are quite intemperate—for example, Charles Ford.

The effect of utilitarian ethics was to replace temperance with prudence. Since self-control is not per se admirable, necessary, possible, or likely, and since things are so arranged that there are natural, social, legal, and religious sanctions to punish misdeeds,[65] virtue becomes identical with prudence—looking out for oneself so as to avoid the "blows and knocks" dealt out by the sanctions, for sinning. Thus prudence supplants temperance, and self-concern (a much more solid base for morals) replaces self-control. And there is greater hope for social peace and order.

At the end of Chapter 2 the point was made that Swift's estimate of the worth of prudence was not clear-cut. As a political writer or orator, he often appeals to what we would call enlightened self-interest—prudence.[66] With all the sanctions (especially legal and religious ones) in operation, the prudent citizen will behave himself: thus prudence is good. But the great and admirable figures of the past and present were generally imprudent—that is, they ignored their own interests, and sometimes the interests of society, out of greatness of mind or virtue, while little piddling spirits prudently followed common forms and succeeded very well.[67] This evidence suggests that Swift's basis of evaluating men is twofold. Sometimes, his judgments, as in the case of prudence, grow out of utilitarian considerations; sometimes, his esteem for heroic behavior and superior character traits (such as courage or magnanimity) seems to result from a concept of human excellence,[68] a rather definite picture of what the highest human type is. It is the purpose of the next chapter to examine this "romantic" side of Swift's ethics.

[65] See John Gay, *Concerning the Fundamental Principle of Virtue or Morality,* reprinted in *The English Philosophers from Bacon to Mill,* ed. E. A. Burtt (New York: Modern Library, 1939), pp. 769–785. Locke's influence on utilitarianism and the general principles of it are discussed with full documentation by A. P. Brogan, "John Locke and Utilitarianism," *Ethics,* LXIX (January, 1959), 79–93.

[66] Bishop Butler calls this "cool self-love" and finds it a legitimate kind of egoism —see his first sermon, "Upon Human Nature."

[67] C, III, 41–42; PW, VIII, 138–139. Often Swift means by *prudence* simply a kind of political wisdom, a good attribute (PW, IX, 185).

[68] That some critics would decide he had no belief in the possibility of human excellence seems to have been anticipated by Swift. In the first edition of *Gulliver's Travels* Swift used the term *Virtue* (which has a meaning that easily slides through a reader's mind) in one place, but later corrects it to the more unavoidable *Perfection* (PW, XI, 132, 307).

CHAPTER 4

Romantic Virtue

To speak of romantic virtue in a study of Swift's ethics would seem to most Swiftians a foolish paradox. Swift is widely understood to be the antiromantic nonpareil, especially in his poetry, where (according to many readers) he attempts to destroy all notions of the worth in human things. This critical error, I believe, has resulted from a generous impulse: to find some excuse for Swift's reputed scatology and coprophobia (or coprophilia). While much intense thought, as well as ink, has been spent in connection with that dark side of the moon, many of the quite visible features of the fair side have been overlooked. Certainly it is clear that Swift was hard on many imperfections of human beings; much that he says does not exalt our species. But his private papers, many of his letters, even his political writings, and especially his poems reveal that he set a very rigorous ethical standard for mankind, and that he was even sanguine about the men who have met, and who can and will meet such a standard. Bolingbroke recognized this characteristic of Swift's ethics: "The truest reflection, and at the same time, the bitterest satire, which can be made on the present age, is this, that to think as you think," he wrote to Swift, "will make a man pass for romantic" (C, III, 25).

I

THE DIGNITY OF HUMAN NATURE

Although there never was a tougher-minded anthropologist than Swift, he had the virtue of the tough-minded: clear-sightedness—clear-sightedness even into the real worth of the romantic:

> . . . although we are apt to ridicule the sublime Platonic Notions they [the nobility in the reign of Charles I] had, or personated, in Love and Friendship, I conceive their Refinements were grounded upon Reason, and that *a little Grain of Romance* is no ill Ingredient to preserve and exalt *the Dignity of human Nature,* without which it is apt to degenerate into a Thing that is sordid, vicious, and low. (PW, IV, 95; italics mine)

The dignity of human nature! The occurrence of such a phrase is almost sufficient ground for a presumption of spuriousness of the work from which it is quoted (*Hints toward an Essay on Conversation,* PW, IV, 87–95). But in earlier pieces Swift had betrayed the same romanticism: to engage in party politics to the destruction of principles and decency is, he argued, "below the Dignity both of human Nature, and human Reason" (PW, I, 233). In *The Examiner* he clearly reveals the psychological effect of measuring poor performance by high standards: ". . . nothing can well be more mortifying than to reflect, that I am of the same Species with Creatures [the Whig journalists] capable of uttering so much Scurrility, Dulness, Falshood, and Impertinence, to the Scandal and Disgrace of Human Nature" (PW, III, 171–172).

Even before his death, however, readers began convincing themselves that Swift's writings, not the subjects of his writings, contributed to "the Scandal and Disgrace of human Nature." It often suited his moral-satiric purposes to mortify man's pride in order to get better performance (at any rate, so he vainly thought). But this truth has blinded readers to another, that Swift often sought to exalt the dignity of human nature in order to spur on those men who can achieve the highest virtue, heroic virtue.

Whether Dr. Johnson was more pessimistic than Swift was hardly an academic question in Boswell's day, for he records the perceptive verdict of Lady McLeod, who asked Johnson "if no man was naturally good." Johnson replied, "No, Madam, no more than a wolf." Boswell puckishly asked, "Nor no woman, sir?" Johnson's answer was no, and Lady McLeod "started, saying low, 'This is worse than Swift'."[1]

As far as human capacities for goodness, for virtue, are concerned, Johnson is several degrees more pessimistic than Swift; he even makes Swift's optimism, absurd to him, a kind of subtheme in his "Life of Swift." Johnson finds Swift's *Project for the Advancement of Religion and Morals* "hopeless, as it supposes more zeal, concord, and perseverance than a view of mankind gives reason for expecting" (251).[2] Johnson shows himself much more certain of the relentless decay and change in human things: of Swift's proposal for an academy to prevent or slow down corruptions of the English language, Johnson says:

> The certainty and stability which, contrary to all experience, he thinks attainable, he proposes to secure by instituting an academy; the decrees

[1] James Boswell, *Boswell's Journal of a Tour to the Hebrides,* ed. F. A. Pottle and C. H. Bennett (New York: Viking, 1936), p. 170.
[2] I give references within the text, in this paragraph only, to Johnson's *Life.*

of which every man would have been willing, and many would have been proud to disobey, and which being renewed by successive elections, would in a short time have differed from itself. (253)

And, in reaction against the biographers who stressed the high-mindedness of Swift's political actions, Johnson protests, "His disinterestedness has been likewise mentioned; a strain of heroism which would have been in his condition romantic and superfluous" (255). But, as will be clear later in this chapter, Swift romantically believed in heroes, and therefore could believe in imitating them.[3]

Swift could never calmly accept the "limits" of human nature and human life, where there is much to be endured. He wrote to a friend, "The public corruptions in both kingdoms allow me no peace or quiet of mind" (C, V, 431). Swift is highly critical of his own jeremiads: ". . . my rage is so ignoble, that is descends even to resent the folly and baseness of the enslaved people [the Irish] among whom I live" (C, IV, 135; cf. 33–34). And, now and then, he makes statements which I fear Johnson would call cant: "It is the mistake of wise and good men, that they expect more reason and virtue from human nature, than, taking it in the bulk, it is in any sort capable of" (TS, XI, 179).

> All Men of Principle . . . have entirely agreed [in not believing a slanderer] . . . which I observe with a great deal of Pleasure, as it is for the Honour of Humane-kind. But as neither Virtue nor Vice are wholly engross'd by either Party [Whig or Tory], the good Qualities of the Mind, whatever Byass they may receive by mistaken Principles, or mistaken Politics, will not be extinguish'd. . . . Men of Honour will always side with Truth. (PW, VI, 176)

The virtue which Swift regarded as pure or heroic was that which was unalloyed with selfish considerations, unassociated with interest: "I love them [the Dutch] for the love they have to their country; which, however, is no virtue in them, because it is their private interest, which is directly contrary in England" (C, V, 64). That an action is contrary to selfish interests is the strongest proof that it is virtuous. Oxford and Bolingbroke (so Swift thought) worked to secure the Hanoverian succession: ". . . which was in them so much a greater mark of virtue and loyalty, because they perfectly well knew, that they should never receive the least mark of favour, when the succession had taken place" (PW, VII, xxxvi).[4] Of virtue thus conceived there is an inevitable shortage,

---

[3] W. B. C. Watkins, in seeking to identify the beliefs of Swift and Johnson, overlooks their differences, *Perilous Balance* (Princeton: Princeton University Press, 1935), pp. 41–48.

[4] See C, II, 383; PW, III, 172; PW, VII, 4. When Steele asserts that in resigning

although "sometimes there may be a peck of it in Asia, and hardly a thimbleful in Europe" (C, IV, 77).

II

MAGNANIMITY: COURAGE, INTEGRITY, HUMANITY

The actions Swift thought virtuous would surely make a select list, such in fact as has survived in a manuscript by Swift, first published after his death: "Of Those who have made Great Figures in some Particular Action of their Lives." This remarkable list deserves to be quoted in entirety, especially since it is generally ignored:

> Alexander the great, after his Victory (at the Streights of Mount Taurus) when he entered the Tent where the Queen and Princesses of Persia fell at his feet.
> Socrates, the whole last Day of his Life, and particularly from the Time he took the Poison to the Moment he expired.
> Cicero when he was recalled from his Banishment. The People, through every place he passed meeting him with Shouts of Joy and Congratulation, and all Rome coming out to receive him.
> Regulus when he went out of Rome attended by his Friends to the Gates, and returned to Carthage according to his Word of Honor, though he knew he must be put to a cruell Death, for advising the Romans to pursue their War with that Commonwealth.
> Scipio the Elder when he dismissed a beautiful Captive Lady, presented to him after a great Victory, turning his Head aside, to preserve his own Virtue.
> The same Scipio, when he and Hannibal met before the Battle; if the Fact be true.
> Cincinnatus when the Messengers, sent by the Senate to make him Dictator, found him at the Plow.
> Epaminondas when the Persian Ambassador came to his House and found him in the midst of Poverty.
> The Earl of Strafford the Day that he made his own Defence at his Tryall.
> King Charles the Martyr during his whole Tryall, and at his Death.
> The Black Prince when he waited at Supper on the King of France, whom he had conquered and taken Prisoner the same Day.
> Virgil, when at Rome the whole Audience rose up, out of Veneration, as he entered the Theatre.
> Mahomet the great when he cut off his beloved Mistress's head on a

---

his appointment during the Tory Administration he acted "by Justice and Truth, and Benevolence to Mankind," and "out of Charity to his Country, and to contend for Liberty," Swift will not allow him a claim to "so Romantick a Virtue" and argues that Steele knew he was about to lose his employments anyway and that "his Resignation would be an Appearance of Virtue cheaply bought" (PW, VIII, 20–21); that is, Swift would not allow Steele a claim to romantic virtue, which is not a virtue one can affect; it must be completely unselfish.

Stage erected for that purpose; to convince his Soldiers, who taxed him for preferring his Love to his Glory.

Cromwell, when he quelled a mutiny in Hyde-Park.

Harry the Great of France, when he entered Paris, and sate at Cards the same Night with some great Ladyes, who were his mortal Enemyes.

Robert Harley Earl of Oxford, at His Tryall.

Cato of Utica, when he provided for the Safety of his Friends, and had determined to dy.

Sir Tho More during his Imprisonment, and at his Execution.

The Earl of Oxford when he was stabbed by Guiscard.

Marius when the soldier sent to kill him in the Dungeon was struck with so much aw and Veneration that his sword fell from his Hand.

Douglas when the ship he commanded was on Fire, and he lay down to dy in it, because it should not be said that one of his Family ever quitted their Post.

Sr Jerom Bows. (PW, V, 83–84)

The manuscript thus breaks off; but it is not hard to guess what particulars would have followed the name of Sir Jerome-Bowes, the fiercely courageous ambassador appropriately sent by Queen Elizabeth to the court of Czar Ivanvasilovitch. I would suggest, as would any one after reading the ancedotes in the *DNB* article on Bowes by R. C. Browne, that after Bowes' name Swift would have written:

> . . . when, after the French ambassador's hat was nailed to his head, for his not removing it before the Czar, he attended the next audience with his hat on his head; and replied to the Czar's asking, whether he had heard what happened to the Frenchman, by saying that he did not represent the cowardly King of France, but the invincible Queen of England, "who does not vail her bonnet nor bare her head to any prince living."

There can be little doubt that Swift admired precisely Bowes' courage, especially in view of the fact that of the nineteen men listed (two of them twice), seventeen (thus excluding Virgil and Cicero) were famous either for their general bravery or for the brave act to which Swift refers in each case. Of the particular actions, rather than the men, fourteen of the twenty-one concern great courage—whether the fierce boldness of Bowes; the military bravery of Cromwell and Douglas; the tranquil, cheerful, indifferent fearlessness of Socrates and Marius; the brilliant, courageous self-possession of Strafford; or the romantic courage of Charles at his execution.

In these actions, and clearly in those of Scipio and Regulus, is a courage of "conviction," an adherence to principle, to honor or to duty to one's country or one's friends—or, if you will, the fear of something worse than death, whether that something is dishonor, craven selfishness, or violation of principle. Scipio, before the battle of Zama, refused to accept the easy peace offered by Hannibal, because it was dishonorable to Rome, which had not started the war. Hannibal's fear of ill-fortune contrasted with Scipio's declaration that he preferred death and defeat to dishonorable peace; the interview closed with Scipio saying, ". . . prepare for war as you have been unable to endure peace."[5] Regulus' action which Swift notes was much more virtuous: a Roman commander captured by the Carthaginians, he was forced to go to Rome to sue for peace; bound by oath to return to Carthage, where he was to die if peace was not made, he nonetheless advised his countrymen in Rome to continue the war. Swift explains this type of courage, which he seems to have regarded as the basis of all other virtues,[6] in one of his last pamphlets: ". . . a Man of Courage, [is] not to be drawn from his Duty by the Frowns or Menaces of Power, nor capable to be corrupted by Allurements or Bribes" (PW, XIII, 70). Of a similar nature is the courageous devotion or faith of Sir Thomas More, whom Swift elsewhere declared to be "a person of the greatest virtue this kingdom ever produced" (PW, XIII, 123).

The kind of courage that Swift most wondered at, probably because it was not one of his own attributes, was intrepidity, as in the case of Socrates, Marius, Harry the Great, and Harley. At the end of the War of the Three Henrys, Henry of Navarre conquered Paris and became Henry IV (Harry the Great); he visited several ladies who had vowed to kill him, showing them great kindness (by assuring them their estates were safe) and trust (by taking some light repast with them, whereby he could easily have been poisoned).[7] Intrepidity is the right term for this kind of courage, since the beauty of it inheres in not showing the least fear or concern (in *not trembling*) in the face of certain death or in the most dangerous adventures. *Intrepid* is the term that Swift applied to Harley (PW, VII, 19); and intrepidity is in the main the principal element in the magnanimity which Swift believed Harley displayed when Guiscard attacked him, in the midst of a hearing, with a penknife:

> I hope [Harley's enemies] will at least admire his Magnanimity, which is a Quality esteemed even in an Enemy. . . . After the Wound was given, he was observed neither to change his Countenance, nor discover any Concern or Disorder in his Speech: He rose up, and walked along the Room while he was able, with the greatest Tranquility, during the Midst of the Confusion. . . . [picking up the knife, he said] he thought it now

[5] Livy, *The History of Rome*, XXX, xxxi. I quote from the Everyman edition.
[6] See P, I, 6–7.
[7] See H. D. Sedgwick, *Henry of Navarre* (Indianapolis: Bobbs Merrill, 1930), pp. 232–234.

properly belonged to him. He shewed no Sort of Resentment, or spoke
one violent Word against Guiscard; but appeared all the while the least
concerned of any in the Company. A State of Mind, which in such an
Exigency, nothing but Innocence can give; and is truly worthy of a
Christian Philosopher. (PW, III, 109)

A few years later Harley's behavior during the unsuccessful prosecution
for treason before the hostile House of Lords earned Swift's praise:
"Lord Oxford confounds them with his intrepidity" (C, II, 293).[8]

Probably even greater magnanimity Swift found in the career and,
especially, in the last day of Cato the Younger, who together with Brutus
represents what Swift regarded as the greatest human type: the magnanimous patriot, who will risk all for the welfare of his country and
friends (or, like Socrates, for philosophy; or More, for his faith). Quite
naturally, in Swift's thinking, courage is the key principle of greatness
of soul. The extent of one's courage is the acid test. If one is brave
enough to die in the name of virtue, or for one's country, then surely
his action has finally no truly selfish basis. The patriot who sacrifices
himself for his country embodies the highest possible virtue. Courage, in
the form of indifference to death, is not only the proof of one's truly
heroic worth, but also something like the necessary cause of good actions.
That concept of courage is a consequence of Swift's view of human life,
in which a few gifted, worthy men are confronted by general viciousness.[9] As I noted earlier, to deal honestly with the knavishly inclined
is to invite personal disaster; thus, only those who will run the risk of
misfortune, the brave, will act virtuously.[10] The only base for the highest
action is fearlessness, even in the face of death (although a necessary
element in virtue is also integrity, or indifference to money). Swift's
heroes knew how to die: Socrates, Strafford, Charles I, Cato, Sir
Thomas More, Marius, Douglas, Brutus, and also Harley: "It hath
pleased me . . . to hear that he preserved the greatness and calmness and
intrepidity of his mind to his last minutes, for it was fit that such a life
should terminate with equal lustre to the whole progress of it"; "Lord
Oxford died like a great man" (C, III, 197, 202).[11]

---

[8] Swift thought Stella's courage remarkable, too: "She thinks that Nature ne'er
design'd / Courage to Man alone confin'd" (P, II, 725); see the following lines also.
"She had the personal courage of a hero" (TS, XI, 130).

[9] See Irvin Ehrenpreis's discussion of this point in *The Personality of Jonathan
Swift,* (London: Methuen, 1958), pp. 59 ff.

[10] See Chapter 2.

[11] "Here is an ingenious good-humoured physician, a fine gentleman, an excellent
scholar, easy in his fortunes, kind to everybody, has abundance of friends, entertains
them often and liberally. They pass the evening with him at cards, with plenty of
good meat and wine, eight or a dozen together. He loves them all, and they him.
He has twenty of these at command. If one of them dies, it is no more than 'poor

Swift's magnanimous man, however, is not simply brave; he is also a man of integrity—by which Swift meant indifference to wealth, freedom from avarice, incorruptibility (C, I, 266, 280). In the list of great figures the two striking examples of integrity are Cincinnatus and Epaminondas. Cincinnatus was the proverbial example of original, old-fashioned Roman simplicity, frugality, elemental existence. Epaminondas was the Theban general who was able to lead Thebes to the heights of its glory. According to Plutarch, when Epaminondas died he had only one iron coin and had therefore to be buried at public expense. Famed for his philosophy and honored politically, he lived by choice in poverty all his life. He and Pelopidas shared power in the state and army without friction: "The true cause of this was their virtue; whence it came that they did not make their actions aim at wealth and glory, an endeavor sure to lead to bitter and contentious jealousy; but both from the beginning being inflamed with a divine desire of seeing their country glorious, by their exertions, they used to that end one another's excellences as their own." Like Harley, Epaminondas underwent an unjust trial for capital crime: "Epaminondas bore the accusation very patiently, esteeming it a great and essential part of courage and generosity not to resent injuries in political life."[12] Also, to Swift, William Sancroft (P, I, 33 ff.), Joseph in the Old Testament, Socrates, Sir Thomas More, Brutus, and Cato were great examples of incorruptibility.

Magnanimity also entails humanity and generosity, as in Alexander's treatment of the women of Darius and in Scipio's release of the captive lady. To be magnanimous is to be above the little vices and ignoble actions which can be committed with impunity, and to avoid the ordinary by strength of will. Cruelty is expected in the conqueror, but not found in Alexander's courtesy, or in Edward's (the Black Prince's) treatment of the French King whom he had defeated and captured: rather Edward showed the King greater honor and hospitality, and insisted on waiting on him at dinner, saying that "he was not worthy to sit at table with so great a king or so valiant a man."[13] There is an element of humility in Swift's concept of greatness of soul.

Tom'! He gets another, or takes up with the rest, and is no more moved than at the loss of his cat. He offends nobody, is easy with everybody. Is not this the true happy man? . . . I would give half my fortune for the same temper, and yet I cannot say I love it" (C, IV, 58–59). He wrote to Oxford: ". . . both religion and reason forbid me to have the least concern for that lady's [Oxford's daughter's] death" (C, II, 88).

[12] Plutarch, *The Lives of the Noble Grecians and Romans,* tr. John Dryden, rev. Arthur Hugh Clough (New York: Random House, n.d.), pp. 231, 349, 360, 730.

[13] See the *DNB* article on Edward by W. Hunt. There can be little doubt that Swift regarded humility as a rare and great virtue (J, I, 275; PW, VIII, 133). See

The magnanimous man is above taking a petty revenge.[14] As will be clear in the discussion of Cato and Brutus, below, he is able to ignore his own misfortune while acting for the welfare of his associates. And he may achieve a superhuman indifference to anything which might make death easier, as when Sir Thomas More refused to take any wine before his execution; this resembles a little the Stoic state of *apathia,* an almost cheerful calm—consider, for example, More's joking with the executioner about his beard, which (he said) had never committed treason.

The "great figures" made by Socrates, Strafford, Charles I, Henry the Great, Harley, More, Marius, Cato, and Brutus constitute a kind of triumph of virtue, even in the face of victory by their enemies or opponents. By their heroism they achieve a greater victory in losing so magnificently or magnanimously. The justice of such achievement must have drawn Swift's attention, notably in the two "figures" of Cicero and Virgil—one being the triumph of political virtue, the other the triumph of poetic talent.

III

ROMAN VIRTUE

Cato and Brutus are great examples not only of the magnanimity that Swift admired, but also of what he praised as "Roman virtue." To remind the scholarly world that a neoclassical writer like Swift held the patriots of Rome in the highest esteem is to carry coals to Newcastle. But when a historical or biographical truth becomes commonplace, its complexity is often ignored, its vitality impaired. And, if the current of history obscures what was clear in Swift's time—if the knowledge of the history of Rome and Greece which was a part of every educated man's mind in Swift's day has almost no existence today—then there is a great chance for oversight and underestimation.

For many centuries Cato's name had almost magical overtones. Plu-

---

the end of Section I in Chapter 5, where Aristotle's understanding of magnanimity, sometimes called pride, is discussed. I cannot here attempt to give an account of the difference between Christian and pagan notions of magnanimity. The definitions of two virtues in Milton's *De Doctrina Christiana* are illuminating: "Lowliness of mind consists in thinking humbly of ourselves, and in abstaining from self-commendation except where occasion requires it"; "Magnanimity is shown, when in seeking or avoiding, the acceptance or refusal of riches, advantages, or honors, we are actuated by a regard to our own dignity, rightly understood"—and Milton points to the example of Christ, "rejecting the empire of the world." See *The Student's Milton,* ed. F. A. Patterson (New York: Appleton-Century-Crofts, 1933), pp. 1064–1065.

[14] See his remark on hindering many bitter things against Marlborough, "because I thought it looked base" (J, II, 597).

tarch's biography is an almost poetic telling of the grandeur of his life; and some of the magic may still subsist, even in our own day.

On a superficial level Cato's career sounds a little like Swift's. He often engaged in violent exercise, lent money without interest, wrote some rather scurrilous verses; he was rigorously honest in all his public capacities and ready to die for the liberty of his country, by which he meant ready to defend it against any kind of tyrannic rule: ". . . though he was terrible and severe as to matters of justice, in the senate and at the bar, yet after the thing was over his manner to all men was perfectly friendly and humane"; too many instances of his absolute fearlessness are on record for that ever to be doubted. As Swift noted, never did Cato's excellences reveal themselves more clearly than on the day of his death. Siding with Pompey against Caesar, Cato had gone to Africa and there joined Scipio, Pompey's father-in-law, who was subsequently defeated in a crucial battle by Caesar. All was lost for Cato and his friends. He took the greatest care to provide for the safety of his men in their escape by sea. After a philosophical banquet Cato read Plato's *Phaedo* twice, slept soundly a few hours, woke, checked again on some of the men who were late in sailing, and avoided the ignominy of capture by Caesar, the Roman way: killing himself with his sword.[15]

There is no mystery, then, in Swift's respect for Cato, whom (as he says), "I esteemn to have been the wisest and best of all the Romans" (PW, II, 2); or, together with Brutus, he praises as one of the "two most virtuous Men in Rome" (PW, VI, 133–134); or, with Socrates, as "the two instances, wherein [the virtues of temperance and fortitude] arrived at the greatest height" (PW, IX, 249). Swift's friend Sheridan, who also honored the ancients, and his housekeeper, Mrs. Whiteway, paid him the compliment of a comparison with Cato, whom (as I have suggested) he resembled in some ways.[16]

The Swift-Bolingbroke correspondence furnished just the necessary coloring and depth to Swift's admiration of Cato. Scholars lately have been "on to" something in the intellectual disagreement between Swift and Bolingbroke. The usual interpretation is that Swift the Christian opposed Bolingbroke the Deist. Somehow, Deism and nothing else in the eighteenth century equals classicism; and therefore Bolingbroke was more a classicist than Swift.[17] But there were many philosophies in clas-

[15] Plutarch's *Lives,* pp. 918–960. Are Cato's severity and humanity mirrored in those stoical animals, the Houyhnhnms?

[16] C, V, 316–317; VI, 97. The editor, Ball, seems to err in his interpretation of Sheridan's letter.

[17] See, for example, Ehrenpreis, *The Personality of Jonathan Swift,* pp. 99 ff.; and Kathleen Williams, *Jonathan Swift and the Age of Compromise* (Lawrence: University of Kansas Press, 1958), pp. 154 ff.

sical antiquity, about as many as Bolingbroke had sets of convictions, which depended on whether he had political hopes and ambitions or only the consolation of gentlemanly friendship and epicurean contemplation. Clearly, Swift's basic principles in some ways contravened Bolingbroke's, but not in so simple a way as Christianity versus Deism. A part of this disagreement is revealed in their respective assessments of Cato's character. Swift evidently praised Cato in a letter (not now extant) to Bolingbroke, and got this reply:

> Cato is a most venerable name [Bolingbroke wrote]. . . . This Cato . . . strikes me with no great respect. . . . I call to mind that image of him which Tully gives in one of his letters to Atticus, or to somebody else; where he says, that having a mind to keep a debate from coming on in the senate, they made Cato rise to speak, and that he talked till the hour of proposing matters was over. . . . The censor [Cato the Elder] used sharp medicines, but, in his time, the patient [Rome] had strength to bear them. The second Cato inherited this receipt without his skill; and like a true quack, he gave the remedy, because it was his only one, though it was too late. He hastened the patient's death; he not only hastened it, he made it more convulsive and painful. (C, III, 91–92)[18]

In Bolingbroke's next letter we discover again the partial contents of one of Swift's: "You call Tully names, to revenge Cato's quarrel; and to revenge Tully's, I am ready to fall foul of Seneca," whom Swift evidently had quoted against Tully (C, III, 110). On the same day Bolingbroke wrote to Charles Ford:

> I am glad to have so good a Second as you in my quarrel with the D: about Cato. I mean the Second. he was a Cynick in polliticks, & did oftner harm than good, of which I could produce some flaming instances. enough to prove that he liv'd a fanatick & dy'd an Enthusiast. a pretty character for the Saviour of a Common Wealth, whose circumstances were so nice, and whose case was so desperate, that the greatest dexterity imaginable could hardly have gone about to cure without irritating the disease & precipitating the Patients death. (LF, 235)

Perhaps this confrontation needs explication. Surely Swift and Cato both were Cynics in politics (actually, Cato is usually, and Swift occasionally, called a Stoic;[19] and the Cynics, of course, were historically the

---

[18] Bolingbroke here agrees with Machiavelli, who also thought politics a highly complicated science; see his *Discourses,* Book III, Chapter I.

[19] A modern critic like Ehrenpreis can assume that Deism equals Stoicism and that Deism (for Swift) equals Bolingbroke, *The Personality of Jonathan Swift,* pp. 99 ff. Something is awry, however, for Bolingbroke disliked the Stoics and affirms that he agrees with them in *one* particular, that a good man should participate in politics (C, III, 110). Bolingbroke was aware of the closeness of Stoicism to Christianity (see C, III, 110), and he declares his favorite philosopher to be Aristippus—who was *not,* however, a Stoic (C, III, 111).

close cousins or brothers of the Stoics). Uncapitalized *cynicism* usually suggests today the habit of seeing the worst in everything. But Cynicism considered as one of the permanent philosophical phenomena in Western Civilization is not so simple. At its best, Cynicism is an absolutist humanitarian ethical philosophy, whose adherents have no use whatsoever for compromised goods. Many of the Cynics in antiquity were highminded, philanthropic public servants—for example, Crates, Cercidas, Demetrius, and Demonax.[20] Like Cato, they refused to engage in political compromise and sophisticated refinements, but rather sought the straight, honest way. They were inflexibly good, incorruptible. Bolingbroke had no respect for such rigorists (and probably a healthy fear of them); he saw politics more as a game of shifting powers, in which the flexible, intelligent leader (a skillful surgeon) can by clever compromise and adroit maneuver give necessary direction to a society's movement in history, direction as much toward the good as the society's "health" can stand. Traditionally, the Cynics considered themselves as physicians to man, but they did not think that a physician's function was to pamper man in his vices. Rather it was to cure him of them altogether.[21]

As one of "the two most virtuous Men in Rome," by Swift's evaluation, Brutus is of almost identical virtue as Cato. Today, however, Brutus is robbed of some of the honor earlier paid to him, as a result either of Shakespeare's characterization or of recent interpretation of Shakespeare's characterization.[22] According to Plutarch, Brutus made two mistakes,—in sparing Antony and in letting him order a funeral for Ceasar,—both of which were the errors of a generous nature;[23] Shakespeare, I would judge, changed Plutarch's evaluation little (as anyone can see in Antony's final speech in the play), except perhaps to add a touch of the melancholic Elizabethan intellectual to Brutus' character.

Modern opinion, however, is not the point. Brutus lived and died enough a hero to command the respect of his enemies. Even Antony thought that his actions were completely unselfish and honorable:

[20] D. R. Dudley, *A History of Cynicism* (London: Methuen, 1937), pp. 42–53, 74–84, 125–135, 159–161.

[21] *Ibid.,* p. xii.

[22] See, e.g., Tucker Brooke's views on *Julius Caesar* in *A Literary History of England,* ed. A. C. Baugh (New York: Appleton-Century-Crofts, 1948), p. 527: "For the understanding of the average playgoer [Shakespeare] allows Brutus to remain the idealistic hero that Plutarch called him; but he had inward doubts which a careful and repeated reader of the play begins to share; while Cassius, so clearly slated for the villain's part, refuses to maintain that status and ends by robbing his colleague of much of our sympathy."

[23] Plutarch's *Lives,* pp. 1197–1198.

> This was the noblest Roman of them all:
> All the conspirators save only he
> Did that they did in envy of great Caesar;
> He only, in a general honest thought
> And common good to all, made one of them.
> His life was gentle, and the elements
> So mix'd in him that Nature might stand up
> And say to all the world "This was a man!"[24]

He was the great example, to Swift and many others, of the patriot who hated tyranny and loved the liberty of his country; in fact, he and Swift held the same view of political liberty: government by law and not by arbitrary personal will.[25] Brutus, it should be noted, was also a gentle, philosophic man; as such, he differed from his tyrannicide ancestor, Junius, who was famous for:

> . . . his courage and resolution in expelling the Tarquins and destroying the monarchy. But the ancient Brutus was of a severe and inflexible nature, like steel of too hard a temper, and having never had his character softened by study and thought, he let himself be so far transported with his rage and hatred against tyrants that, for conspiring with them, he proceeded to the execution of his own sons.[26]

In his first political pamphlet Swift shows a preference for Brutus' courage and integrity, rather than for Cicero's somewhat timorous accommodation to the powers that were:

> . . . when Cicero wrote to Brutus, how he had prevailed by his credit with Octavius, to promise him [Brutus] Pardon and Security for his Person; that Great Roman received the Notice with the utmost Indignity, and returned Cicero an answer [yet upon Record] full of the highest Resentment and Contempt for such an Offer, and from such a Hand.

It is not clear whether the next sentence refers to the advent of the Caesars or the end of the Brutuses: "Here ended all Shew, or Shadow, of Liberty in Rome" (PW, I, 222). Less serious is a little anecdote in the *Journal to Stella,* concerning a conversation with a man named Cesar:

> We happened to talk of Brutus, and I sd something in his Praise, when it struck me immediately that I had made a Blunder in doing so, and therefore I recollected my self & sd, Mr. Cesar I beg your pardon. (J, II, 602)

[24] *Julius Caesar,* V, v, *The Complete Works of Shakespeare,* ed. Hardin Craig (Chicago: Scott Foresman, 1951), p. 796.
[25] See Irvin Ehrenpreis' careful study, "Swift on Liberty," *JHI,* XIII (April, 1952), 131–146.
[26] Plutarch's *Lives,* pp. 1187, 1204.

These considerations can further work to solve one of the few remaining puzzles in Swift's biography, as Herbert Davis has explained it in his edition of *The Drapier's Letters*: "If there is any special significance in the letters M. B. [the Drapier's initials] . . . no one appears yet to have discovered it."[27] *M. B.*, I suggest, stands for Marcus Brutus, and is thus another of Swift's incongruous jokes as well as a hieroglyph for the Drapier's (and Swift's) hatred of tyranny and oppression.[28]

With such patriots as Cato and Brutus, to consider only the most illustrious, no wonder is it that the Romans elicited from Swift the praise that they were "the noblest People that ever entered upon the Stage of the World" (PW, I, 212), or that he referred repeatedly to them in all questions of political policy (see PW, I, 195 ff; XII, 183; C, III, 121). It would be paradoxical indeed if the author of *The Battle of the Books* did not hold such views, not only of respect for Rome and Greece, but also of rhapsodic admiration of the whole "Current of Antiquity" (PW, IV, 27). Strangely enough, some scholars tend to ignore or depreciate this predilection in Swift, probably because it is one that this century does not share.[29] Swift consistently expressed a somewhat amazed admiration for the ancients who were able to make heroic self-sacrifices. They were, in fact, one of his favorite topics, oddly enough, especially in his writings to or about Vanessa and Stella. In *Cadenus and Vanessa*, he condemned "present Times" which have:

> . . . no Pretence
> To Virtue, in the Noblest Sense,
> By Greeks and Romans understood,
> To perish for our Country's Good. (P, II, 697)

And Vanessa either learned her lesson well or anticipated these lines in a letter to Swift:

> Lord! how much we differ from the ancients, who used to sacrifice everything for the good of the commonwealth, but now our greatest men will, at any time, give up their country out of pique, and that for nothing. (C, II, 47)

Today these attitudes seem out of place in a clergyman, but in Swift's age most educated men saw little tension between Christian morals and

---

[27] *The Drapier's Letters,* ed. Herbert Davis (Oxford: Clarendon, 1935), p. 186.
[28] See my note "The Drapier's Initials," *Notes and Queries,* X (June, 1963), 217–218.
[29] See, e.g., K. Williams, *Swift and the Age of Compromise:* of Swift's writings, she finds the *Battle of the Books* the "least interesting" (p. 122). And Miriam Starkman, who has studied Swift's early satires with great care, states at the beginning and end of her study that the cause of the ancients is lost. *Swift's Satire on Learning in "A Tale of a Tub"* (Princeton: Princeton University Press, 1950).

classical ethical philosophy, or tended to ignore it. A fair example, I would say, of the eighteenth-century combination of Christian virtues and classicism is to be found in Fielding's Parson Adams, whose piety is as unquestionable as his knowledge and admiration of the Greek dramatists. But Swift speaks directly of this tension in his sermons, where he often admires the great examples of antiquity:

> . . . scarcely to be believed, or even conceived, in such a base, corrupted, wicked age as this we live in. In those times it was common for men to sacrifice their lives for the good of their country, although they had neither hope or belief of future rewards; whereas, in our days, very few make the least scruple of sacrificing a whole nation, as well as their own souls, for a little present gain; which often hath been known to end in their own ruin in this world, as it certainly must in that to come. (PW, IX, 233) [30]

Yet Swift saw that this conviction in the extreme implies that "either all Revelation is false, or what is worse, that it hath depraved the nature of man" (PW, IX, 242); and he argued for the superiority of religion-inspired morals (see Chapter 5). But it is as far from the truth to say that Swift was an anti-classicist Christian, as to call him an anti-Christian classicist:

> Before you enter into the common unsufferable Cant, [Swift might well advise twentieth-century critics] of taking all Occasions to disparage the Heathen Philosophers; I hope you will differ from some of your Brethren [clergymen], by first enquiring what those Philosophers can say for themselves. . . . I am deceived, if a better Comment could be any where collected upon the moral Part of the Gospel, than from the Writings of those excellent Men. . . . To return then to the Heathen Philosophers: I hope you will not only give them Quarter, but make their Works a considerable Part of your Study. To these I will venture to add the principal Orators and Historians, and perhaps a few of the Poets: By the reading of which, you will soon discover your Mind and Thoughts to be enlarged, your Imagination extended and refined, your Judgment directed, your Admiration lessened, and your Fortitude increased. All which Advantages must needs be of excellent Use to a Divine, whose Duty is to preach and practise the Contempt of human Things. (PW, IX, 73–76)

It is in Swift's poetry, so highly regarded today as excellent in its anti-romantic kind, that one finds repeated, clear-cut instances of his belief in the existence of Roman or romantic virtues. To put the matter simply, Swift's poetry has at least three modes: the well-recognized antiroman-

---

[30] Cf. PW, IX, 135: ". . . how cometh it to pass, that the antient Heathens, who had no other Lights but those of Nature and Reason, should so far exceed us in all manner of Virtue, as plainly appears by many Examples they have left on record?"

tic or mock-heroic (satiric or burlesque); the heroic or sublime; and
the lyric (in the sense that Horace's *Odes* are lyric). In his earliest
poems, the Pindaric odes, Swift supposedly struck an idealistic or Platonic note which was never heard again.[31] For example, in the "Ode
to the King" great enthusiasm is expressed for the Romans, who gave:

> To Valour and to Virtue the same Word:
> To shew the Paths of both must be together trod,
> Before the Hero can commence a God. (P, I, 6–7)

The heroic hyperbole is as unrelieved in his "Ode to Sir William
Temple":

> The mighty Conquest's left to you,
> The Conquest and Discovery too:
> Search out this Utopian Ground,
> Virtue's *Terra Incognita,*
> Where none ever led the Way. (P, I, 26)

> Those mighty Epithets, Learn'd, Good, and Great,
> Which we ne'er join'd before, but in Romances meet,
> We find in you at last united grown.
> You cannot be compar'd to one,
> I must, like him that painted Venus' Face,
> Borrow from every one a Grace;
> Virgil and Epicurus will not do,
> Their courting a Retreat like you,
> Unless I put in Caesar's Learning too,
> Your happy Frame at once controuls,
> This great triumvirate of Souls. (P, I, 28)

It is significant that in the "Ode to Sancroft," after praising Sancroft's
Christian humility and piety, simple goodness, and courage, Swift did
not finish the poem, which thus ends on the statement that "Heaven
and Cato both are pleas'd" (P, I, 42) with Sancroft's character and
career. Surely this is a metaphysical conceit—and a strange way to
praise a Christian!

The heroic mode, however, does not die with the early odes, at least
insofar as Swift's sentiments of heroic virtue are concerned; in an imitation of Callimachus, Swift praised Lord Carteret:

> Once on a Time, a righteous Sage
> Griev'd at the Vices of the Age,
> Apply'd to Jove with fervent Prayer;
> "O Jove, if Virtue be so fair

[31] Ricardo Quintana, *The Mind and Art of Jonathan Swift* (London: Oxford
University Press, 1953), p. 36. For a tracing of platonism or idealism in Swift's later
poems, see Ronald Paulson, "Swift, Stella, and Permanence," *ELH,* XXVII (December, 1960), 312.

> As it was deem'd in former Days
> By Plato, and by Socrates,
> (Whose Beauties mortal Eyes escape,
> Only for want of outward Shape)
> Make thou its real Excellence
> For once the Theme of human Sense.
> So shall the Eye, by Form confin'd,
> Direct, and fix the wandring Mind,
> And long-deluded Mortals see,
> With Rapture, what they wont to flee." (P, II, 383–384)

In view of the efforts of Swift scholars to place him in the traditions of the late Renaissance,[32] we can perhaps refine on their efforts, by noting C. S. Lewis' explanation of the way that the Renaissance poet looked at virtue: "His aim is indeed ethical as well as aesthetic. . . . But this is part of the loveliness, for virtue is lovely, not merely obligatory; a celestial mistress, not a categorical imperative."[33]

The heroic shades into the lyric, perhaps, in Swift's limitations of Horace: to Oxford in the Tower he directs these lines:

> How blest is he, who for his Country dies;
> Since Death pursues the Coward as he flies.
> . . . .
> Virtue repuls't, yet knows not to repine;
> But shall with unattainted Honour shine;
> . . . .
> Virtue, to crown her Fav'rites, loves to try
> Some new unbeaten Passage to the Sky;
> Where Jove a Seat among the Gods will give
> To those who die, for meriting to live. (P, I, 210)

No clearer evidence of the extent to which Swift's ethical thought was conditioned by Roman examples and doctrine can be found than in the Horatian imitations (since they not only parallel Horace's thought, but also imitate Swift's own sentiments, as expressed elsewhere).[34] Whatever his erstwhile differences with Archbishop King, Swift was ready to praise him in a Roman manner when he courageously (along with Swift) opposed the British policy related to Wood's halfpence:

> The Man, who Infamy to shun,
> Into the Arms of Death would run,
> That Man is ready to defend
> With Life his Country, or his Friend. (P, I, 243)

[32] Quintana, *Mind and Art,* pp. 59 ff.; Ronald Paulson, *Theme and Structure in Swift's Tale of a Tub* (New Haven: Yale University Press, 1960). 28 ff.

[33] C. S. Lewis, *English Literature in the Sixteenth Century* (Oxford: Clarendon Press, 1954), p. 322.

[34] The poem to Harley is a close rendering of Horace, *Odes,* III, 2, "Call to Youth."

> Great, good, and just was once apply'd
> To One who for his Country died.
> To One who lives in its Defence
> We speak it in a Happier Sense. (P, I, 339)

In a general way, such views epitomize the Roman understanding of political virtue, and in particular they echo Horace's (*Odes*, IV, 9): the *vir beatus*:

> ... deems dishonor worse by far than death;
> For friends and country yields his latest breath,
> Living for them, he dares for them to die.[35]

Even in less public poems, the "romantic" tone is sustained, as in the following lines from poems to Vanessa and Stella. To Vanessa, he offers:

> ... Friendship in its greatest Height,
> A constant, rational Delight,
> On Virtue's Basis fix'd to last. (P, II, 711)

To Stella:

> Heroes and Heroins of Old
> By Honour only were enroll'd
> Among their Brethren of the Skies,
> To which (though late) shall Stella rise. (P, II, 725)

> ... Virtue, stil'd its own Reward,
> And by all Sages understood,
> To be the Chief of human Good. (P, II, 764)

> ... is not Virtue in Mankind
> The Nutriment that feeds the Mind?

> . . . .

> ... Virtue in her daily Race
> Like Janus, bears a double Face;
> Looks back with Joy where she has gone,
> And therefore goes with Courage on. (P, II, 765)

These lines apparently show that, for Swift, virtue had not become "ideal" in modern times, that it was achievable by private as well as public persons; as do also his comments on Temple, Sir Thomas More, Berkeley, Arbuthnot, the Scot Montrose, William Sancroft, the Bishop of Marseilles, even an English politician (William Pulteney), and an Irish mayor (Humphrey French).[36] In his unfinished "Abstract of the

---

[35] *The Works of Horace,* ed. C. J. Kraemer (New York: Random House, 1936), p. 290.
[36] P, I, 33 ff.; C, III, 218, 262, 278; C, V, 107, 143, 177, 321, 418; C, VI, 58–59; PW, XIII, 85; TS, X, 345; TS, XI, 318–319.

History of England" Swift pays careful attention to the virtues and vices of the few kings that he discusses; the highest praise, however, goes to the brother of Queen Maud,[37] Robert, Earl of Gloucester:

> ... than whom there have been few private persons known in the world that deserve a fairer place and character in the registers of time, for his inviolable faith, disinterested friendship, indefatigable zeal, and firm constancy to the cause he espoused, and unparallelled generosity in the conduct thereof: he adhered to his sister in all her fortunes, to the ruin of his own; he placed a crown on her head; and when she had lost it by her folly and perverseness refused the greatest offers from a victorious enemy, who had him in his power, and chose to continue a prisoner rather than recover his liberty by any hazard to her pretentions: he bore up her sinking title in spite of her own frequent miscarriages, and at last died in her cause by a fever contracted with perpetual toils for her service. An example fit to be shewn the world, although few perhaps are like to follow it; but however, a small tribute of praise, justly due to extraordinary virtue, may prove no ill expedient, to encourage imitation. (PW, V, 65)

IV

THE GREAT PARENT OF VIRTUE

Swift placed the blame for the shortage of virtue in his day partly on the inadequacies of modern education, which, he thought, was "always the worse in Proportion to the Wealth and Grandeur of the Parents"—in other words, the complete reverse of the practice of the ancients: "... a Scholar may fill half his Greek and Latin Shelves with Authors of the noblest Birth as well as highest Virtue" (PW, XII, 46). The fault of modern education, Swift also thought, is that it begins with wrong principles, such as this, that "the Study of Greek and Latin is Loss of Time" (PW, XII, 48).[38] Swift's thinking here needs emphasis: there is little virtue nowadays because those who could achieve the most get the worst education and because the most useful knowledge, that of the history and literature of Greece and Rome, is not taught:

> There is one Circumstance in a learned Education, which ought to have much Weight, even with those who have no Learning at all. The Books read at Schools and Colleges, are full of Incitements to Virtue, and Discouragements from Vice, drawn from the wisest Reasons, the strongest Motives, and the most influencing Examples. Thus, young

[37] She and her cousin Stephen were struggling for control of England.

[38] This is the tendency of Hobbes' opposition to the classics: see *Leviathan*, Chapters XXI, XXIX, XLVI. Locke also did not see the necessity in a gentleman's being forced to learn classical languages: *Some Thoughts concerning Education* in *The Works of John Locke*, 10th ed. (London: Bye & Law, 1801), Nos. 147 ff.

Minds are filled early with an Inclination to Good, and an Abhorrence
of Evil; *both which increase in them, according to the Advances they
make in Literature.* (PW, XII, 52; italics mine)

One of Hobbes' pronouncements, because of its speciousness, continually drew Swift's fire:

. . . the Romans [Hobbes writes in *Leviathan*] . . . were taught to hate
monarchy, at first, by them that having deposed their sovereign, shared
amongst them the sovereignty of Rome; and afterwards by their successors. And by reading of these Greek, and Roman authors [such as
Aristotle and Cicero], men from their childhood have gotten a habit,
under a false show of liberty, of favouring tumults, and of licentious
controlling [controverting] the actions of their sovereigns, and again of
controlling those controllers; with the effusion of so much blood, as I
think I may truly say, there was never any thing so dearly bought, as
these western parts have bought the learning of the Greek and Latin
tongues.[39]

In one of his several responses to this statement, which is the opposite of
Swift's almost religious reverence of classical antiquity, Swift makes a
telling criticism of Hobbes' political philosophy:

Arts and Sciences took their Rise, and flourished only in those few small
Territories where the People were free. . . . *Arbitrary Power* [which
Hobbes believed to be the only alternative to anarchy] is but the *first*
natural Step from Anarchy or the Savage Life; the adjusting of Power
and Freedom being an Effect and Consequence of *maturer* Thinking.
(PW, II, 18; italics mine)

Swift believed that one did *not* in any way "imbibe ill Opinions, from
reading the Histories of ancient Greece and Rome, those renowned
Scenes of Liberty and every Virtue" (PW, XII, 278; cf. also PW,
VIII, 37; XII, 161). He even advises a young woman newly married
to learn to relish conversation about the "great Men and Actions of
Greece and Rome" (PW, IX, 91).

The men and actions of antiquity inspire one with a spirit of emulation,[40] which, even in rivalry for fellowships at a university (C, V, 124)

[39] *Leviathan*, XXI (141).
[40] "Emulation is pain caused by seeing the presence, in persons whose nature is
like our own, of good things that are highly valued and are possible for ourselves to
acquire; but it is felt not because others have these goods, but because we have not
got them ourselves. It is therefore a good feeling felt by good persons, whereas envy
is a bad feeling felt by bad persons. . . . It is accordingly felt by the young and by
persons of lofty disposition. . . . since all good things that are highly honoured are
objects of emulation, moral goodness in its various forms must be such an object,
and also all those good things that are useful and serviceable to others" (II, 11);
see Aristotle's *Rhetoric and Poetics*, tr. W. R. Roberts and Ingram Bywater (New
York: Random House, 1954), p. 120. For Swift's opinion of Aristotle: "Aristotle's

or among clergymen generally, is "the legal Parent of the greatest Virtues and most generous Actions among Men" (PW, XII, 201–202).

It is again in the poetry that Swift speaks with least hesitation and most enthusiasm, this time about the most important cause of virtue: emulation. We know by Swift's own testimony that he knew Stella from her childhood "and had some share in her education, by directing what books she should read, and perpetually instructing her in the principles of honour and virtue; from which she never swerved in any one action or moment of her life" (TS, XI, 127). If we assume that Swift speaks the truth in this last remark, the methods he used in such a moral education must have been happily chosen: consider how he describes his practice and doctrine as a tutor, first to Esther VanHomrigh:

> How was her Tutor wont to praise
> The Genius's of Ancient Days!
> (Those Authors he so oft had nam'd
> For learning, Wit, and Wisdom fam'd;)
> Was struck with Love, Esteem, and Awe,
> For Persons whom he never saw.
> Suppose Cadenus flourish'd then,
> He must adore such God-like Men. (P, II, 708)

He explains to Stella how she must decide all moral questions:

> In Points of Honour to be try'd
> All Passions must be laid aside;
> Ask no Advice, but think alone,
> Suppose the Question not your own:
> How shall I act? is not the Case,
> But how would Brutus in my Place?
> In such a Cause would Cato bleed?
> And how would Socrates proceed?   (P, II, 724)

To a man of Dr. Johnson's cast of mind, such hero worship, such worship of the past, is foolish, according to Mrs. Piozzi's account:

> As ethics or figures, or metaphysical reasoning, was the sort of talk he most delighted in, so no kind of conversation pleased him less I think, than when the subject was historical fact or general polity. "What shall we learn from that stuff (said he)? let us not fancy like Swift that we are exalting a woman's character by telling how she
>
> > Could name the ancient heroes round,
> > Explain for what they were renown'd &c."[41]

Poetry, Rhetorick, and Politicks are admirable" (PW, II, 97); "He . . . seems to be a person of the most comprehensive genius that ever lived" (TS, XI, 185).

[41] Either Dr. Johnson or Mrs. Piozzi does not quote accurately from *Cadenus and Vanessa*; see P, II, 697.

I must not however lead my readers to suppose that he meant to re-
serve such talk for men's company as a proof of pre-eminence. "He
never (as he expressed it) desired to hear of the Punic war while he
lived: such conversation was lost time (he said), and carried one away
from common life, leaving no ideas behind which would serve living
wight as warning or direction."

> How I should act is not the case,
> But how would Brutus in my place?

"And now (cries Mr. Johnson, laughing with obstreperous violence), if
these two foolish lines can be equalled in folly, except by the two succeeding ones—shew them me."[42]

The two succeeding lines (quoted above) are:

> In such a Cause would Cato bleed?
> And how would Socrates proceed? (P, II, 724)

Brutus, Cato, and Socrates represented the heroic tradition of antiquity, which appealed strongly to Swift's mind. He felt that their lives
were models which would encourage, would challenge, those few
human beings who have, or have been given, an inclination to virtue.
Only the fortunate few can accept the challenge; only exceptional men
and women can rise above human nature, can aspire to godlike greatness, superhuman virtue.[43] The scarcity of virtue enhances the achievement; man is a creature *capax rationis* (C, III, 277), which for Swift
means capable of reason, or virtue—just as man is a creature capable
of playing the piano: only a few can do it well. In virtue these few
present, as did Robert, Earl of Gloucester, examples "fit to be shewn the
world, *although few perhaps are like to follow it;* but however, a small
tribute of praise, justly due to extraordinary virtue, may prove no ill
expedient to encourage imitation" (TS, X, 256; italics mine). It was
Swift's prayer that Stella's "many Virtues, as far as human Infirmity
will admit, be our constant Imitation" (IX, 254). In a similar spirit, he
wrote to John Gay's friend, the Duchess of Queensbury: "Pray God
preserve your Grace and family, and give me leave to expect that you
will be so just to number me among those who have the greatest regard
for virtue, goodness, prudence, courage, and generosity" (C, IV, 204).
And his epitaph, his own composition, flings the challenge to the future:

---

[42] *Anecdotes of Samuel Johnson,* ed. S. C. Roberts (Cambridge, England: Cambridge University Press, 1932), pp. 54–55.
[43] It cannot be overstated that virtue to Swift meant exceeding the limits of human
nature: Consider the following lines and their contexts: "He must adore such Godlike Men" (P, II, 708); "Before the Hero can commence a God" (P, I, 6–7);
"Common Forms were not design'd / Directors to a noble Mind" (P, II, 706);
"Else you relapse to Human Kind" (P, II, 724–725).

Abi viator, et imitare, si poteris, strenuum pro virili libertatis vindica-
torem. (PW, XIII, 149)

Go, traveller, and *imitate if you can* one who strove his utmost to champion liberty. [44]

---

[44] Quoted from Middleton Murry, *Jonathan Swift* (London: J. Cape, 1954),
p. 484; italics mine.

CHAPTER 5

Virtue and Interest

By insisting that virtue, in order to be genuine, must be heroic, Swift seems to set the mark of excellence too high for ordinary human beings. If only a few achieve such heroism, the generality of men are without any proper merits, or claims to merit. In academic jargon, only one degree is given, the *summa cum laude,* and only those who earn it graduate; the rest fail.[1] But Swift did not ignore the problem of ordinary, day-to-day citizen virtue and a related subject, public order. Typically, his way of looking at these is that of the legislator, who will establish a public religion and a set of laws which best insure that each citizen is a peaceful asset to the commonwealth.

I

RELIGIOUS INSURANCE

Scholars trying to understand Swift's religious-moral thought have often felt the need to find a clearer or more systematic thinker with whom to compare Swift: variously, Montaigne, Pascal, Hobbes, Locke, Temple, Mandeville, Butler, even Hume.[2] Although it redounds to Swift's honor if we compare him to a great philosopher or a currently popular thinker, a parallel of less eminence may bring more light: for example, between Swift and a conservative Anglican divine, a younger contemporary and modestly successful author, John Brown (1715–1766), who published in 1751 his *Essay on the Characteristics of Lord*

---

[1] I borrow this metaphor from C. S. Lewis.

[2] Montaigne and Locke: Wedel, "On the Philosophical Background of Gulliver's Travels," *SP,* XXIII (October, 1926), 434–450. Pascal: Irvin Ehrenpreis, *The Personality of Jonathan Swift* (London: Methuen, 1958), pp. 99, 109, 114. Hobbes: David P. French, "Swift and Hobbes—a Neglected Parallel," *Boston USE,* III (Winter, 1957), 243–255. Temple: Ricardo Quintana, *The Mind and Art of Jonathan Swift* (London: Oxford University Press, 1953), pp. 15 ff. Mandeville: an unpublished dissertation (Vanderbilt, 1951), "Swift and Mandeville as Critics of Society," by B. R. Rhodes, Butler: James Brown, "Swift as Moralist," *PQ,* XXXIII (October, 1954), 368–387. Hume: Lucius Elder, "The Pride of the Yahoo," *MLN,* XXXV (April, 1920), 206–211.

Shaftesbury. The following is a résumé of the central argument of Brown's anti-Benevolist tract:[3]

Virtue is the "voluntary Production of the greatest public Happiness"—the happiness of others. But the only motive to virtue is "the Prospect of future private Happiness," for what else besides the anticipation of acquiring happiness (pleasure) or avoiding unhappiness (pain) can motivate us? This view has led modern Epicureans (Hobbes, Mandeville, and a few French writers) to see no benevolence and virtue whatever in man: ". . . heaping up a Collection of sordid Instances, which prove the sensual Inclinations and Selfishness of Man, [these writers] leap at once to the desired Conclusion, that the pretended public Affections are therefore no more than the same low Passions in Disguise." But the Stoics, ancient and modern (like Shaftesbury and adherents), "dwell altogether on the social or public" inclinations, or virtues, in man's nature. Thus, "according to one, Mankind are naturally a Race of Demi-Gods; according to the other, a Crew of Devils." But man is a blend of truly social and truly selfish affections. The particular bias of each person depends on his physical constitution and his education. That explains the intellectual disagreement between Mandeville and Shaftesbury. The latter simply had few "sensual Appetites," or very weak ones. Epicureans—for example, Mandeville—are usually "Men of high Health, florid Complexions, firm Nerves, and a Capacity for Pleasure: Of the Stoic Party are the delicate or sickly Frames, Men incapable of the grosser sensual Enjoyments, and who either are, or think themselves, virtuous."

Admittedly, in a few happy constitutions, where "the amiable Affections" are predominant, virtue has "all the Force and Energy" which somewhat pagan moralists like Shaftesbury describe. When the temptations to sensual pleasure are weak, the "moral sense" can operate with authority. To such an amiable (and anemic) person, virtue is truly its own reward, a great pleasure and source of peace. Such persons are scarce, however, if they exist at all. And who will offer insurance that passion will not sometimes break out in the service of self-love?

Every one, it is clear, cannot achieve such an exalted state of virtue, however charming it may be to the moralist "wrapped up in Visions of ideal Perfection." A refined theory of morals has no efficacy in this world, "amidst the Struggle of contending Passions." The moral dreamer may retire from the world and live in innocence, but virtue is the "actual Production of Good": ". . . if we rigorously examine the external Consequences of an active Virtue, in such a World as this; we shall find, it must be often maintained at the Expence both of Health, Ease, and Fortune; often the Loss of Friends, and Increase of Enemies; not to mention the unwearied Diligence of Envy, which is ever watchful and prepared to blast distinguished Merit."

No trust can be placed in human reason, which does little but serve

[3] John Brown, *Essay on the Characteristics of Lord Shaftesbury* (London: C. Davis, 1751), pp. 123–238.

the passions. Honor is no sort of guide for virtue or guarantee of it; for it is always dependent on the opinion of others, who can easily be deceived and thus may honor the dishonorable and condemn the truly honorable. The affective nature of man (his physical constitution), however, is a permanent factor in human action. And much depends on the intensity and ratio of the public and private affections. Also, while man has no innate sense of good or set of instincts to guide him, God has given him a sense of future pain and pleasure, which sense can be exploited for the sake of virtue, by means of sanctions. There are human laws which force a coincidence of private behavior and public good. There is a God who will adjust discrepancies and injustices of human law enforcement, in the afterlife. Thus religion becomes the cause of human virtue most likely to succeed, for religion is grounded in the permanent passions of men (fear of pain, hope of pleasure). It is realistic; it can be universally successful. Religion, it must be admitted, participates nonetheless in the uncertainty of all human things; and at times it is corrupt. But "here and there a happy Nation emerges," where true religion and religion-inspired virtues are found.

Brown's political or utilitarian Christianity is remarkably close to Swift's, when Swift speaks as a clergyman.[4] Both make virtue political, but Brown uses utilitarian language, Swift uses Roman (virtue is love of one's country).

The crucial question for both is *how one can with great success insure the existence of virtue.*

As does Brown, Swift thinks that there is no security in what men call honesty. Some people, Swift argues in one of his sermons, "who appear very indifferent as to Religion," gain a reputation of moral honesty; they have the reputation of being good men. Yet a man who is good on such a basis may do some wrong, for his motivation is rooted in his "own Ease and Interest," and if "he hath nothing to govern himself by, but the Opinion of the World, as long as he can conceal his Injustice from the World, he thinks he is safe" (PW, IX, 152).

Nor is "Honour," as it is understood in modern times, enough: "It is true indeed, that in ancient Times it was universally understood, that Honour was the Reward of Virtue" only. But now what is called honor keeps very few from doing anything immoral. And honor often motivates men to bad actions, by which they unjustly gain renown (PW, IX, 153–154).

Swift considers the moral teaching of the ancients, where honor was given such a high role as motive to virtuous action:

---

[4] Swift apparently made a distinction between speaking as a clergyman and not: see C, III, 81; V, 339.

. . . how cometh it to pass, that the ancient Heathens, who had no other Lights but those of Nature and Reason, should so far exceed us in all manner of Virtue, as plainly appears by many Examples they have left on record?

The answer he finds is that the ancients gave their children a strict education and that the best of them also taught that there is an afterlife where the virtuous will be rewarded, the vicious punished (PW, IX, 155–156).

The possibility of the success of pagan schemes of morality poses a threat to Christian morals. Which is more "excellent," pagan or Christian ethics? With his usual courage and forthrightness, Swift states the question: ". . . either all Revelation is false, or what is worse, . . . it hath depraved the nature of man" (PW, IX, 242).

His sermon "Upon the Excellency of Christianity" is in part an argument that pagan ethics do not afford adequate social security and peace of mind. First, he raises some objections against pagan schemes: since the ancients could not agree on a chief good,[5] they engaged in vain "disputes about words." Further, "to say, as the most plausible of them did, that happiness consisted in virtue, was but vain babbling, and a mere sound of words" (PW, IX, 242–244). But Swift's main point is that their ethics "wanted some suitable reward." He explains that "human nature is so constituted, that we can never pursue any thing heartily but upon hopes of reward." He then turns to the ancients, to see how their ethics accommodated this characteristic of human nature:

> . . . some of the philosophers gave all this quite another turn, and pretended to refine so far, as to call virtue its own reward, and worthy to be followed only for itself: Whereas, if there be any thing in this more than the sound of words, it is at least *too abstracted to become an universal influencing principle in the world, and therefore could not be of general use.* (PW, IX, 244; italics mine)[6]

When the ancients, especially the Stoics or Cynics, talked of enduring pain simply because such endurance is noble and frees a man from the lower concerns of life, they are not admirable:

[5] Locke makes the same point in a witty way in his *Essay concerning Human Understanding* in *The Works of John Locke,* 10th ed. (London: Bye & Law, 1801), II, 21, No. 58.
[6] The change of focus from the heroic to the general is clear here. See also Berkeley's *Alciphron,* where pagan ethics is called "too sublime and enigmatical"; "sublime and speculative"; and in general unlikely to sway "men of cool heads and close reason," *The Works of George Berkeley,* ed. A. A. Luce and T. E. Jessop (Edinburg: T. Nelson, 1948–1957), III, 121, 130, 134.

To talk of bearing pain and grief, without any sort of present or future hope, cannot be purely greatness of spirit; there must be a mixture in it of affection, and an allay of pride, or perhaps it is wholly counterfeit. (PW, IX, 245)

Further, the ancients, Swift argues, without revealed religion, had no valid "notions of a Deity," and were also without the solace of a belief in providence (PW, IX, 245). Swift brings a group of charges against several ancient philosophers, all of whom, in one way or another, found the virtuous man to be in need of the goods of fortune. Thus, for example, Solon's philosophy could not salve the death of his son; Aristotle said that the good man is not happy without wealth and health. In the Christian scheme, however, providence and the afterlife, Swift points out, make sickness and death and poverty momentary inconveniences which the good man can endure with hope and peace of mind (PW, IX, 246–247).

The Christian dispensation is much more just; wise and good men suffer for their virtue in this world, and expect recompence only in the next. The pagan concept of fortune left the good man at the mercy of all the ills of life, without a farther or higher hope of succor beyond his own virtue. The Christian scheme brought relief, hope, and justice for the good, who get less than they deserve in this world.[7]

There is then no public security in virtues based on moral honesty, or honor, or any nonreligious ethics; which is as much as to say that no law which a man gives himself, or which is made for him and enforced by some human authority, will suffice for public order:

> Suppose a Man thinks it his Duty to obey his Parents, because Reason tells him so, because he is obliged by Gratitude, and because the Laws of his Country command him to do so: But if he stops here, his Parents can have no lasting Security; for an Occasion may happen, wherein it may be extremely to his Interest to be disobedient, and where the Laws of the Land can lay no hold upon him. (PW, IX, 154)

Any moral tie not founded in religion cannot withstand the pressures of Interest—". . . the Pride, or Lust, or Avarice, or Ambition of Mankind" (PW, IX, 158). Virtue alone, or even with the shabby support of reason and civil law, is almost defenseless against Interest and its powerful friends, Pride, Lust, Avarice, Ambition. The political, the social, the religious problem is to find powerful friends for virtue, to get some real

---

[7] Swift is uninformed or does not care to speak about the relationship of late Stoicism to Christian doctrine.

strength on the right side. The problem is to join interest with virtue, in the name of safety or security.[8]

That religion[9] alone can join virtue and interest is the argument of Swift's sermon "On the Testimony of Conscience," which begins with a definition of *conscience,* as signifying "that Knowledge which a Man hath within himself of his own Thoughts and Actions. And . . . if a Man judgeth fairly of his own Actions by comparing them with the Law of God, his Mind will either approve or condemn him according as he hath done Good or Evil" (PW, IX, 150). That is, conscience is a purely cognitive faculty, almost identical with what we would today call consciousness. Swift intended, no doubt, to rule out any suggestion of the cognitive-intuitive authority such as Bishop Butler saw in the conscience, or (to connect him with an earlier Christian tradition which includes many of the Church Fathers and St. Thomas Aquinas) such as Milton describes as the law of God "engraven upon the mind of man."[10] Locke had intimidated divines and moralists by his criticism of the notion of innate ideas,[11] and Hobbes, Locke, and Swift are all examples of the tendency of the Enlightenment to distrust the voice from within, or inspiration, so well satirized by Samuel Butler in *Hudibras:*

> Whate'er men speak by this new light,
> Still they are sure to be i' th' right.
> 'Tis a dark-lanthorn of the spirit,
> Which none see by but those that bear it. (I, 503–506)[12]

Yet Swift seems to have believed that if ethical knowledge is not innate in man, it is available to him, learned or not:

> The Inconstancy of Fortune, the Goodness of Peace, the Excellency of Wisdom, the Certainty of Death; that Prosperity makes Men insolent, and Adversity humble; and the like eternal Truths, . . . every Plowman knows well enough, although he never heard of Aristotle or Plato. (PW, IX, 76)

He clearly believed that men who are honest and honorable (that is, who overcome any tendency to bias or prejudice or selfish partiality)

---

[8] Thus the virtue which results is not pure or heroic; see Chapter 4. Swift tends to speak of joining *duty* and interest, rather than *virtue* and interest—which would indicate a shift, too.

[9] Swift hardly stresses the point that it is revealed religion. See the discussion concerning Deism in Chapter 9.

[10] John Milton, *The Christian Doctrine,* I, xi. I quote from *The Student's Milton,* ed. F. A. Patterson (New York: Appleton-Century-Crofts, 1933), p. 996.

[11] Traditional thinkers were uneasy after Locke's attack. See Swift's mockery of Locke's nominalism, PW, II, 79–80. Archbishop King wrote to Swift of his deepest convictions in the following way: ". . . when or how I come by them, or whether I was born with them I cannot tell" (C, II, 9).

[12] Samuel Butler, *Hudibras,* ed. H. G. Bohn (London: G. Bell, 1882).

will easily agree in matters of ethics (PW, VI, 176; C, III, 277). Since
ethical knowledge is available, Swift can remark, "I never wonder to
see Men wicked, but I often wonder to see them not ashamed" (PW,
IV, 251): that is, men know what is right, even if they are not able to
avoid wickedness. And Swift seems to have felt that the ancients are not
to be condemned for not having had the benefits of the Gospel. Rather
they are to be admired for having arrived at the ethical truths in it
without revelation, but simply by natural reason (PW, IX, 73). The
more wisdom a man possesses, the more certain he is about ethical
truths:

> I am apt to think, that in the Day of Judgment there will be small Al-
> lowance given to the Wise for their want of Morals, or to the Ignorant
> for their want of Faith; because, both are without Excuse. This renders
> the Advantages equal of Ignorance and Knowledge. But some Scruples
> [in religion] in the Wise, and some Vices in the Ignorant, will perhaps be
> forgiven upon the strength of Temptation to each. (PW, I, 243)

If you will, this ethical knowledge, the main element in what Swift
and his age called reason, is roughly equivalent to common sense:
"Common Reason soon distinguished between Virtue and Vice" (PW,
II, 19; cf. VIII, 44, 47; XII, 22). The idea that agreement is possible
among rational men is fairly strong in Swift: "If a rational Man reads
an excellent Author with just Application, he shall find himself extremely improved, and perhaps insensibly led to imitate that Author's
Perfections" (PW, IX, 76). Thus reason possibly means that faculty,
which, taking a disinterested view of society, can reach conclusions as to
the moral acts necessary for the good of society (PW, IX, 146).[13] But
the trouble, of course, is that men are not disinterested or dispassionate
and, therefore, do not obey reason:

> How often do we contradict the right Rules of Reason in the whole
> Course of our Lives? Reason itself is true and just, but the Reason of
> every particular Man is weak and wavering, perpetually swayed and
> turned by his interests, his Passions, and his Vices. Let any Man but con-
> sider, when he hath a controversy with another, although his Cause be
> ever so unjust, although the World be against him, how blinded he is
> by the Love of himself, to believe that Right is Wrong, and Wrong is
> Right, when it maketh for his own Advantage. Where is then the right
> Use of his Reason, which he so much boasteth of, and which he would
> blasphemously set up to controul the Commands of the Almighty? (PW,
> IX, 166)

Swift nonetheless speaks continually of the rational faculty as properly
(but all too seldom) guiding a man's actions. One of the few faults he

[13] Berkeley argues in the same fashion in *Passive Obedience*.

finds in Stella is that she often lets her passions sway her judgment and
does not wait "Till Time hath open'd Reason's Gate" (P, II, 730);
he thinks emotional preaching shameful and warns a clergyman not to
be too emotional in his sermons: ". . . beware of letting the pathetick
Part swallow up the rational: For, I suppose, Philosophers have long
agreed, that Passion should never prevail over Reason" (PW, IX, 70).

In the same work ("A Letter to a Young Gentleman"), however, he
notes that "Reasoning will never make a Man correct an ill Opinion,
which by Reasoning he never acquired" (PW, IX, 78). And Swift once
quarreled with the more optimistic Richard Steele on this very issue:
". . . he [Steele] affirms, That Men's Beings are degraded when their
Passions are no longer governed by the Dictates of their own Mind;
directly contrary to the Lessons of all Moralists and Legislators; who
agree unanimously, that the Passions of Men must be under the Government of Reason and Law; neither are Laws any other Use than to correct the Irregularity of our Affections" (PW, VIII, 46–47).

Thus, alongside the more traditional statements of the need for the
hegemony of reason are ones which imply that Swift saw more order in
a dispensation wherein reason would cooperate with the passions. This
latter view has some basis in his belief that the passions cannot be
overcome by temperance: "The Stoical Scheme of supplying our
Wants, by chopping off our Desires; is like cutting off our Feet when we
want Shoes" (PW, I, 244); and, further, in his recognition that the
passions are essential elements of human life:

> In a Glass-House, the Workmen often fling in a small Quantity of fresh
> coals, which seems to disturb the Fire, but very much enlivens it. This
> may allude to a gentle stirring of the Passions, that the Mind may not
> languish. (PW, I, 242)

> Although reason were intended by providence to govern our passions,
> yet it seems that, in two points of the greatest moment to the being and
> continuance of the world, God hath intended our passions to prevail
> over reason. The first is, the propagation of our species, since no wise
> man ever married from the dictates of reason. The other is, the love of
> life, which, from the dictates of reason, every man would despise, and
> wish it at an end, or that it never had a beginning. (PW, IX, 263)[14]

In the sermon on conscience Swift assumes that man has knowledge
of good and evil, not because it is innate,[15] but rather because it derives

---

[14] What *reason* means in the last sentence is problematic. Nietzsche speaks of the
"tragic wisdom" of the satyr Silenus, who was caught and forced to reveal the
greatest truths: that it is best never to be born and that it is next best soon to die.
[15] Since conscience is not the voice of God, in Swift's opinion, he has no patience

from experience and revealed religion. Conscience is but awareness of
one's actions and how they are to be judged, in accordance with the
ethical knowledge that one has acquired. Religion does not bring greater
ethical knowledge,[16] but surer ethical motivation: ". . . there is no solid,
firm Foundation of Virtue, but in a Conscience directed by the Principles of Religion" (PW, IX, 154). The first proof that he offers is in the
form of the example discussed above, the duty of obeying one's parents:
before "a Man can safely be trusted" to obey his parents, he must
consider not just his own moral views, and the laws of the land:

> . . . he must proceed farther, and consider, that his Reason is the Gift
> of God; that God commanded him to be obedient to the Laws, and did
> moreover in a particular manner enjoin him to be dutiful to his Par-
> ents; after which, if he lays a due Weight upon those Considerations,
> he will probably continue in his Duty to the End of his Life: *Because
> no earthly Interest can ever come in Competition to balance the Danger
> of offending his Creator, or the Happiness of pleasing him.* And of all
> this his Conscience will certainly inform him, if he hath any Regard to
> Religion. (PW, IX, 154; italics mine)

He who would have men virtuous must make use of "the two greatest
natural Motives"—fear and hope (PW, IX, 155). It is a characteristic
of much ethical thought of the Enlightenment (in the writings, for
example, of Brown, Swift, Hobbes, Locke, and Hume) that the rational
element in human behavior is regarded as capricious and untrustworthy.
What a man may think will vary with his education, the occasion, and
his passions. It is the affective qualities in man which are the constant
elements in human nature; on these qualities must be based any ethics
which hopes to be successful.

The prominence of the passions in human motivation and the other
limitations in human life do not encourage the practice of virtues: a
virtuous man does not always succeed in the world, and the worst
villains often escape punishment:

> But when Conscience placeth before us the Hopes of everlasting Happi-
> ness, and the Fears of everlasting Misery, as the Reward and Punish-
> ment of our good or evil Actions, our Reason can find no way to avoid
> the Force of such an Argument otherwise than by running into Infi-
> delity. (PW, IX, 155)

---

with Puritan or dissenter arguments for liberty of conscience, or liberty to act in
accordance with an "inner voice." Swift explains the meaning of liberty of conscience
as the "Liberty of knowing our own Thoughts" (PW, IX, 151).

[16] The pagans are not held to be wanting a proper knowledge of ethics (their
philosophy is a good commentary on the ethics of the Gospels); rather they wanted
a proper incentive.

It is virtue and not salvation that Swift has in mind when he speaks of "the Divine Sanction which our Saviour gave to his [System of Morality]" (PW, IX, 73).[17]

With divine sanctions Christianity becomes a social or historical organization of great efficacy, and is thus superior in still another way to the ancient moral doctrines: ". . . the great examples of wisdom and virtue, among the Grecian sages, were produced by personal merit, and not influenced by the doctrine of any particular sect; whereas, in Christianity, it is quite the contrary" (PW, IX, 249). Possibly Swift errs in ignoring the intellectual and moral force in the successions of philosophies in antiquity. In any event, he seems convinced that men such as Socrates were virtuous by accident of the "natural dispositions of their own minds" rather than as a result of "the doctrines of any sect they pretended to follow" (PW, IX, 249). Christianity brings a divinely sanctioned doctrine, which achieves a widespread effect in becoming a general social movement through history, influencing millions. The countless early martyrs show the efficacy of Christianity in inspiring "fortitude and patience" in many thousands, not just in a few (PW, IX, 249).

In one instance only is Swift's preference for Christian ethics grounded in a difference in the moral doctrines themselves, as distinguished from the question of the security of each, pagan or Christian. Or, rather, he argues for the superiority of Christian ethics on the basis of a Christian ethical principal: in discussing Stoic *apathia* and Cynic indifference, Swift calls attention to a tincture of affectation and pride. But "the Christian doctrine teacheth us all those dispositions that make us affable and courteous, gentle and kind, without any morose leaven of pride or vanity, which entered into the composition of most Heathen schemes" (PW, IX, 244, 248). Pagan ethics are the ethics of the proud; one of the highest pagan ethical types was the magnanimous man, Aristotle's *megalopsychos* (or to use the term some translators prefer, the *proud man*). The *megalopsychos* was the man who demanded what he deserved. To demand more was to be vain (a vice); to demand too little, to be humble, was a worse vice, according to Aristotle.[18] But Christianity tames the proud; it lays "Restraints on

[17] Swift never speaks, as does John Scott (a clergyman who wrote Swift a letter explaining his plans to publish a book to put an end to schisms forever [C, VI, 141]), about "true religion" which will "appear to consist in the mortification of our bodily and spiritual lusts." Nor does he use terms like *salvation* and *regeneration* in the fashion of canting enthusiasts.

[18] *Nicomachean Ethics*, IV, iii, 15–16, 37.

human Nature" (PW, II, 38)[19] and thus socializes the sometimes fierce animal, man. Religion, when not in decline (as Swift sadly believed it to be in his day), enforces benevolence in man: "We have just Religion enough to make us hate," he wrote at a time of great sectarian controversy, "but not enough to make us love one another" (PW, I, 241).

II
POLITICAL INSURANCE

By *interest* Swift meant some largely permanent attitude toward a good or evil. It is a man's interest, for example, to hope for prosperity, to fear sickness. For the most part, a man's behavior originates in interests, which might be called permanent passions; and knowledge of a man's interests is the best guide to his future behavior. For that reason, in politics, not a man's avowed principals or his conscience, but his interests are "the only Test by which we are to judge the Intentions of those who manage publick Affairs" (PW, VIII, 177). The only "safe Rule" to follow, in political choices, is to find the man or party whose interests are most closely aligned with those of the public (PW, VIII, 179–180):

> If there be any Maxim in Politicks, not to be controuled, it must be the following. That those whose private Interest is united with the Interest of their Country; supposing them to be of equal Understanding with the rest of their Neighbours, will heartily wish, that the Nation should thrive. (PW, XII, 248)

Almost by accident, Swift believed, the interest of the Oxford ministry had "the same Bottom" as the country's, for which reason (he said) he supported that ministry (PW, VI, 133–134; VIII, 85, 144).[20] In particular, Swift believed the ending of the War of the Spanish Succession and the restoration of public prosperity (especially ending the tax burden on property) were in the public interest. Since the war was a Whig undertaking, and since the Oxford ministry stood more aligned with the landed interests, it was the ministry's interest, also, to end the war and ease the tax burden.

Another concrete case illustrates Swift's thinking. In Dublin two men

---

[19] As implied in Swift's attitude toward liberty of conscience, his thinking is anti-libertarian. He heavily satirizes Steele's belief in religious and political freedom, with the usual ironic reduction: ". . . even Women and Children love Liberty; and you cannot please them better than by letting them do what they please" (PW, VIII, 46).

[20] "I follow those who, I think, are most for preserving the Church and State, without examining whether they do so from a principle of virtue or of interest" (C, II, 113).

were standing for the Irish parliament, one an alderman with a royal appointment which brought him four hundred pounds a year. Since the interests of Ireland often necessitated resistance to the crown, Swift argued against the election of the alderman:

> I desire, my Fellow-Citizens, you will please to call to mind how many Persons you can *vouch for* among your Acquaintance, who have so much Virtue and Self-denial, as to lose 400 1. a Year for Life; together with the Smiles and Favour of Power; and the Hopes of higher Advancement, meerly out of a generous Love of his Country. (PW, XIII, 82; italics mine) [21]

This "interest" psychology is an even more basic part of what we may call Swift's political theory, not only with reference to a choice among aspirants for office, but also in connection with the fundamental principles of a country's constitution:

> In all well-instituted Commonwealths, Care hath been taken to limit Mens Possessions; which is done for many Reasons; and among the rest, for one that perhaps is not often considered: Because when Bounds are set to Mens Desires, after they have acquired as much as the Laws will permit them, their private Interest is at an End; and they have nothing to do, but to take care of the Publick. (PW, I, 243)

A humorous anecdote which Swift supposedly related to Mrs. Pilkington makes his meaning clearer: Swift encouraged an Irish bishop to help resist the oppressions of the British. The bishop refused, because he hoped for a better see (which depended on the crown). After he got a better see he still refused, hoping now for an archbishopric, which he got, without any hope of becoming primate. Whereupon, he said to Swift, "I am now ready to turn patriot," and was until his death. Mrs. Pilkington quotes a bit of self-depreciation by Swift, to the same effect: "He thought it a great blessing that all his hopes of preferment were at once cut off [when he became Dean of St. Patrick's] insomuch that he had nothing to tempt or mislead him from a patriotism in which his grateful country found their happiness and security."[22]

Since agriculture is obviously a major undertaking of any country and since the landed tend to take a more conservative, long-range view of the public good (PW, XII, 89; IX, 21), it is in the public interest to encourage agriculture and to give political power to the landed rather than to the moneyed (PW, III, 5):

---

[21] One should note that the man opposing the alderman was Humphrey French, whom Swift praised for his heroic virtue (PW, XIII, 82–83).

[22] *Memoirs of Mrs. Letitia Pilkington,* intr. by Iris Barry (London: G. Routledge, 1928), pp. 45–46.

I ever abominated that scheme of politics, now about thirty years old, of setting up a moneyed interest in opposition to the landed; for I conceived there could not be a truer maxim in our government than this, that the possessors of the soil are the best judges of what is for the advantage of the kingdom. If others had thought the same way, funds of credit and South Sea projects would never have been felt nor heard of. (C, III, 121)

The Tories were to realize the seriousness of the change which Swift regretted, as the gentlemen-farmers began to lose out gradually in the political developments of the eighteenth century. As Deane Swift noted: "I am sure the present generation of men [in 1755], that is the present generation of landed men, who are in fact the only proprietors of the whole kingdom, feel it to their cost, that Swift's reasonings are just, and that all his accounts are true."[23] A recent student of Renaissance humanism in its English development connects a humanistic principle with the policies of the eighteenth-century Tories: this humanism "was closely associated with the political hegemony of the landed gentry. . . . In the middle of the eighteenth century, accordingly, the literary and ethical values of Humanism were employed in the Tory campaign against middle-class commercial and urban values. . . . This was the strategy that informed the writings of Bolingbroke, as well as Swift, Pope, and Gay."[24] As do many of the humanistic principles, this one derives from classical antiquity.[25]

The most sanguine project ever envisaged by Swift (*A Project for the Advancement of Religion*) involves a practical suggestion. Although he asks Queen Anne to do something she could well have done, the optimism on Swift's part has to do with the consequences which he imagined might ensue. The *Project* begins with a few observations on the degeneracy of the present age, a perennial topic of divines, Swift knows, but actually true in this case, ". . . upon a fair Comparison of other Times and Countries" (PW, II, 45). The great difference is that men regard vices as matters of course, to be accepted as "common Occurrences of Life" (PW, II, 45). But a stigma can again be attached to vice, if the Queen wishes:

> . . . while the Prerogative of giving all Employments continues in the Crown . . . it is in the Power of the Prince to make Piety and Virtue become the Fashion of the Age; if at the same Time he would make them necessary Qualifications for Favour and Preferment.

[23] Deane Swift, p. 155.
[24] J. P. Hart, "Viscount Bolingbroke: Augustan Humanist," *Dissertation Abstracts*, XXII, No. 4 (1961), 1177.
[25] See, e.g., Aristotle's *Politics*, VI, ii; and the discussion of the King of Brobdingnag's agrarianism in Chapter 7.

That is, if she will make "it *every Man's Interest* and Honour to cultivate Religion and Virtue" (PW, II, 47; italics mine). Since his argument is directed to the Queen, Swift appeals also to her interest: a great
reformation in religion and morals would "brighten Her Character to
the present and after Ages"; therefore, her "best Endeavours in this
weighty Affair, are a most important Part of Her Duty, as well as of
Her Interest, and Her Honour" (PW, II, 62).

As in the case of the Oxford ministry, discussed above, there is often
a happily accidental juncture of virtue and interest: ". . . the little
Religion there is left in the World hath been observed to reside chiefly
among the middle and lower Sort of People, who are neither tempted to
Pride and Luxury by great Riches, nor to desperate Courses by extreme
Poverty" (PW, IX, 174)—that is, the limits and advantages of their
position insure their piety. And Swift can offer the following consolation
to the poor:

> . . . your Work of Salvation is easier, by your being liable to fewer Temp-
> tations, and as your Reward in Heaven is much more certain, than it
> is to the Rich, if you seriously perform your Duty, for Yours is the King-
> dom of Heaven. . . . the Lowness of your Condition, in a Manner, forceth
> you to what is pleasing to God, and necessary for your daily Support
> [that is, poverty forces them to be temperate and work hard]. Thus your
> Duty and Interest are always the same. (PW, IX, 197–198)

The secret of the success of Swift's political pamphlets, I would suggest, lies in his sober, unemotional appeal to permanent interest. That
is to say, Swift does not titillate the emotions of the reader (see PW, IX,
69–70), but wields what Dr. Johnson thought "the mere weight of
facts" in such a way that the most vital and lasting interests of the
audience are touched (e.g., see PW, VI, 3–65, 77). How clever this
mode of persuasion can be, Swift reveals in one of the *Drapier's Letters,*
where he estimates the number of Wood's halfpence that will be needed
for the ordinary man to buy a quart of ale (PW, X, 12). The drinking
of ale is a minor but permanent interest; and the slightly exaggerated
"weight of facts" made no small impression on the Dublin populace.

As did most political thinkers in England after Hobbes, Swift seems
to place a premium on order and security within a country. One could,
I suppose, classify British thinkers as authoritarian or libertarian, depending on whether they stress public peace and order or individual
rights and security. Hobbes presented a rigorously deduced moral-
political system wherein all moral obligations have reason and existence
because of fear; that is, fear is the passion which inspires human reason

to discover and follow the laws of nature, which are the laws of peace. Man in a state of nature lacks security, is afraid: the first law of nature and all the subsequent ones derive from this fear and the drive for peace: ". . . the first, and fundamental law of nature . . . is to seek peace and follow it."[26] Thus the greatest passion or interest a man has, desire for self-preservation, is aligned with morality. A somewhat similar tack is taken by Locke and the utilitarians who follow him. The basic problem is to get the conjunction of virtue (behavior productive of public happiness) and interest (one's own egoistic concerns). This conjunction is accomplished by means of sanctions: the physical sanctions of nature, social approval and disapproval, civil law, and divine law and judgment in the afterlife.[27]

In the manner of Hobbes, Locke, and the utilitarians, Swift constantly tried to get powerful forces on the side of duty.

III

The Humble and the Public-Spirited

In many of Swift's political and theological arguments is the implication that human nature needs control, containment. Swift's pamphlets against Steele, in particular, betray an authoritarian cast of mind, unsympathetic to the pleas of the rights of conscience and freedom of speech, so often made by dissenters and Whigs (PW, VIII, 6 ff.).[28] If pride or a restless viciousness dominates man, the happiness of society necessitates firm control. Anything which tames and civilizes such an untrustworthy animal as man has great social utility. Such a taming force is Christianity, which lacks the affectation and pride of pagan morals and inspires "all those dispositions that make us affable and courteous, gentle and kind" (PW, IX, 248). The moral teaching of Christianity exalts humility and meekness as great virtues; the consolation and hope offered by Christianity is suited to the needs of the poor and humble, not the prosperous and proud:

> Blessed are the poor in spirit: for theirs is the kingdom of heaven. . . .
> Blessed are the meek: for they shall inherit the earth. (Matt. 5:3, 5)

As a pastor, Swift did not teach the poor of his flock so gentle a doctrine:

---

[26] *Leviathan,* XIV (85).
[27] See A. P. Brogan, "John Locke and Utilitarianism," *Ethics,* LXIX (January, 1959), 79–93.
[28] Compare Swift's views with Milton's in *Areopagitica.*

. . . your Work of Salvation is easier, by your being liable to fewer
Temptations; and as your Reward in Heaven is much more certain,
than it is to the Rich, *if you seriously perform your Duty,* for Yours is
the Kingdom of Heaven; so your Neglect of it will be less excusable, will
meet with fewer Allowances from God, and *will be punished with double
Stripes.* (PW, IX, 197; italics mine)

Whereas Swift's apologists have often sought to prove there was no
apostasy in his switch from the Whigs to the Tories in 1709 and 1710,
little attention is given to the real or ostensible changes[29] in his politics
after he returned to Ireland in 1714 and became the champion of Irish
rights and liberty against British oppression. The apparent changes are
the ones to be expected when a man's point of view switches from that
of a governor to that of the governed. As a governor, his interest lay in
policy and modes of persuasion to be used in effecting such policy; as a
citizen, as an oppressed citizen, he tended to think more of liberty and
rights; and the body of citizens became not a mass to be kept pacified,
but an instrument to be wielded against the oppressor. "A Panegyric on
Dean Swift," by the Dean, takes notice of the development:

> When J[onatha]n was great at Court,
> The Ruin'd Party made his Sport,
> Despis'd the Beast with many Heads [the demos],
> And damn'd the Mob, whom now he leads.
> But Things are strangely chang'd since then,
> And Kings are now no more than Men. (P, II, 498)

As Swift's involvement in Irish problems grew, his public as well as
private utterances came closer to the Whig views which he criticized in
Steele, as can be seen in the deepening tinge of his republicanism, which
in Rome as well as in England meant government by a portion of the
citizenry who call themselves free men and who hate despotic power in
one man. However, Swift also understood by republican liberty public
order based on law rather than on the despotic will of one or more
men.[30] He could even praise the Scots for their republicanism, their
being "a brave people and defenders of their liberty" (C, IV, 111).

As did the American founding fathers, who were under the spell of
Locke's philosophy, Swift began to speak more urgently of the rights of
a people to govern themselves or to be governed only by laws to which
they consent (PW, IX, 19; XII, 6); in a sermon he asserts that "in

[29] See, however, Ronald Paulson's argument that when the Harley ministry fell,
"the Swiftian persona shifted easily and naturally from the Horatian to the
Juvenalian," "Swift, Stella, and Permance," *ELH,* XXVII (December, 1960), 305.
[30] See Irvin Ehrenpreis' study, "Swift on Liberty," *JHI,* XIII (April, 1952),
131–146. It should be noted that Swift, unlike Steele, never argued for freedom of
the press, of speech, of conscience, or of religion.

those Countries that pretend to Freedom, Princes are subject to those Laws which their People have chosen" (PW, IX, 144). Out of extreme sensitivity to the injustice of the British domination of Ireland, Swift was led by his patriotism to call for daring and punishable action:

> I am so incensed against the oppressions from England [he wrote a London publisher, Benjamin Motte] and have so little regard to the laws they make, that I do, as a clergyman, encourage the merchants both to export wool and woolen manufactures to any country in Europe, or anywhere else, and conceal it from the Customhouse officers, as I would hide my purse from a highwayman, if he came to rob me on the road, although England hath made a law to the contrary; and so I would encourage our booksellers here to sell your authors' books printed here, and send them to all the towns in England [contrary to British law]. (C, V, 339)

Two centuries earlier a public-spirited Italian had called for even bolder action, to free Italy from its bondage; and both Machiavelli and Swift believed that virtue was love of one's country and public spirit.

After his return to Ireland, and in his increasing occupation with political matters, Swift soon came to hate the very characteristic of the Irish which, he felt, exposed them to continued exploitation by the English: namely, their slavish nature:

> Remove me from this land of slaves
> Where all are fools, and all are knaves
> Where every knave & fool is bought
> Yet kindly sells himself for nought. (P, II, 421)

The Irish had almost no love for their country, Swift believed, no "public spirit" (PW, X, 91; XII, 116); one problem facing the Drapier in his efforts to quash the Wood's halfpence scheme was the very "Lowness of Spirit" of his fellow citizens (PW, X, 53). Swift despised "the Laziness, Ignorance, Thoughtlessness, squandering Temper, slavish Nature, and uncleanly Manner of Living in the poor Popish Natives" (PW, IX, 209) and laid the blame on the

> Aegyptian Bondage of cruel, oppressing, covetous Landlords, . . . who grieve and envy when they see a Tenant of their own in a whole Coat, or able to afford one comfortable Meal in a Month, *by which the Spirits of the People are broken, and made for Slavery.* (PW, IX, 201; italics mine) [31]

---

[31] "I cannot but highly esteem those gentlemen of Ireland, who with all the disadvantages of being exiles and strangers, have been able to distinguish themselves by their valour and conduct in so many parts of Europe, I think above all other nations, which ought to make the English ashamed of the reproaches they cast on the ignorance, the dulness, and the want of courage, in the Irish natives; those defects,

Strange it is that Swift, who had often spoken of putting restraints on human nature, should regret the loss of spirit, or a certain kind of pride, in men.[32] When the Duchess of Queensbury, feeling that Gay had been wronged by the English Court, dared to solicit subscriptions for his new play even from the king and queen, she was "forbid the Court" (see C, IV, 69–70). Her action drew applause of an interesting kind from Swift, who believed himself to be living in a land of slaves: "I would be contented with the worst Ministry in Europe to live in a Country which produces such a spirit as that Girles" (LF, 129).

A nagging question in Swift's mind was why modern citizens lacked public spirit:

> . . . love of our Country, was in antient times properly known by the name of Virtue, because it was the greatest of all virtues, and was supposed to contain all virtues in it: And Many great examples of this virtue are left us on record, scarcely to be believed, or even conceived, in such a base, corrupted, wicked age as this we live in. In those times it was common for men to sacrifice their lives for the good of their country. (PW, IX, 233)

His heroes, discussed in Chapter 4, were men of such virtue—public-spirited, courageous, unselfish. Swift's admiration of antiquity and his consequent hatred of much of modernity gave an odd twist to his Christianity: consider only how quickly, in his sermon, the Christian injunction "love thy neighbor" becomes "be public-spirited" (PW, IX, 232 ff.).

In the words *humility* and *spiritedness* themselves are conflicting notions. Can one prefer an ethic which produces meek and humble men and yet admire the products of an ethical system based on pride and spiritedness, such as those of the ancients? Machiavelli raised the same question:

> Reflecting now as to whence it came that in ancient times the people were more devoted to liberty than in the present, I believe that it resulted from this, that men were stronger in those days, which I believe to be attributable to the difference of education, founded upon the difference of their religion and ours. For, as our religion teaches us the truth and the true way of life, it causes us to attach less value to the honors and possessions of the world; whilst the Pagans, esteeming those

---

whenever they happen, arising only from the poverty and slavery they suffer from their inhuman neighbours, and the base corrupt spirits of too many of their chief gentry, etc. By such events as these, the very Grecians are grown slavish, ignorant, and superstitious," (C, IV, 328).

[32] Speaking of himself, Swift wrote to Pope: ". . . a man of spirit is too proud to be vain" (C, III, 118).

things as the highest good, were more energetic and ferocious in their actions. We may observe this also in most of their institutions, beginning with the magnificence of their sacrifices as compared with the humility of ours, which are gentle solemnities rather than magnificent ones, and have nothing of energy or ferocity in them, whilst in theirs there was no lack of pomp and show, to which was superadded the ferocious and bloody nature of the sacrifice by the slaughter of many animals, and the familiarity with this terrible sight assimilated the nature of men to their sacrificial ceremonies. Besides this, the Pagan religion deified only men who had achieved great glory, such as commanders of armies and chiefs of republics, whilst ours glorifies more the humble and contemplative men than the men of action. Our religion, moreover, places the supreme happiness in humility, lowliness, and a contempt for worldly objects, whilst the other, on the contrary, places the supreme good in grandeur of soul, strength of body, and all such other qualities as render men formidable; and if our religion claims of us fortitude of soul, it is more to enable us to suffer than to achieve great deeds.

These principles seem to me to have made men feeble, and caused them to become an easy prey to evil-minded men, who can control them more securely, seeing that the great body of men, for the sake of gaining Paradise, are more disposed to endure injuries than to avenge them.[33]

It would be a mistake to let the Machiavellian word be the only one; consider the same phenomenon in another perspective. In Graham Greene's novel *The Power and the Glory* there is a whiskey-priest who accepts the slavish squalor of the Mexicans and who gives them hope and consolation. He is opposed by an idealistic, socialistic police lieutenant, who hates the rich and the slavishness of the poor Mexicans. A scrap of their conversation puts the question in the sharpest focus. The priest says:

"You hate the rich and love the poor. Isn't that right?"
"Yes."
"Well, if I hated you, I wouldn't want to bring up my child to be like you. It's not sense."
"That's just twisting ..."
"Perhaps it is. I've never got your ideas straight. We've always said the poor are blessed and the . . . rich are going to find it hard to get into heaven. Why should we make it hard for the poor man too?"

Perhaps it is erroneous to find two principles antagonistic which Swift was able apparently to reconcile. Machiavelli himself at least pretended to make pagan virtue harmonize with Christian beliefs:

[33] Machiavelli, *Discourses*, II, ii. I quote from *The Prince and the Discourses*, ed. Max Lerner (New York: Random House, 1950), pp. 284–285.

... if we were to reflect that our religion permits us to exalt and defend our country, we should see that according to it we ought to love and honor our country, and prepare ourselves so as to be capable of defending her.

Thus Machiavelli could conclude that one of the causes of the dearth of public spirit in Italy was not Christianity, but a "false interpretation of our religion."[34]

Although his "banishment" to Ireland brought out Swift's classical or "Machiavellian"[35] inclinations, his mind from the beginning managed to accommodate both admiration for the ancients and belief in Christian doctrines. Late in his career he could write a poem in which St. Patrick chides the Irish in the manner of a Roman censor:

> Discourag'd Youths, now all their Hopes must fail,
> Condemn'd to Country Cottages and Ale;
> To foreign Prelates make a slavish Court,
> And by their Sweat procure a mean Support;
> Or, for the Classicks read th' Attorney's Guide;
> Collect Excise, or wait upon the Tide.
>
> . . . .
>
> I scorn thy spurious and degenerate Line. (P, III, 793–794)

Many years earlier Swift had explained the complexity of his opinions to Lord Somers:

> ... having been long conversant with the Greek and Roman authors, and therefore a lover of liberty, I found myself much inclined to be what they called a Whig in politics; and that, besides, I thought it impossible upon any other principle, to defend or submit to the Revolution: But, as to religion, I confessed myself to be a High-churchman. (PW, VIII, 120)

It is perhaps idle to inquire which was finally topmost—classical republican virtue or Christianity. That his ethical principles comprised both is clear from the beginning of his career. In 1692 he wrote an ode to a Christian hero, William Sancroft, the nonjuror and onetime Archbishop of Canterbury, to whose career Swift gave this paradoxical praise: "Heaven and Cato both are pleas'd" (P, I, 42).

---

[34] *Discourses*, II, ii (p. 286).
[35] *Machiavellianism* is here used in the honorific sense of "patriotism," "public-spiritedness." See Chapter 7 for a discussion of Swift's opposition to Machiavellianism in the pejorative sense.

PART II

Gulliver's Travels: The Moral Equation

CHAPTER 6

Gulliver Telemachus

Although *Gulliver's Travels* is not a treatise on moral or political philosophy, it belongs to a genre which perforce deals with moral and political questions. As a satire, *Gulliver's Travels* inevitably concerns shades of wisdom and folly, heroics and knavery. We find in it the pre-occupations of Swift's letters and other writings: the evils of faction, the value of kindness, the hypocrisy of human pretensions, the endurance of pride, the prevalence of injustice, the follies of the intellect, the ideals and animality of man.

Given the purpose of satire—to denigrate, to put down, bad things—two means to this end are available: (a) associating or identifying the bad with the repulsive and disgusting (such is the method of *Mac Flecknoe*) or (b) setting it up in contrast with the truly virtuous (as in *Joseph Andrews*). Even in satire seemingly devoid of the second method —for example, that of Aristophanes or Juvenal—the good things are always clearly implied. Human thought and language are such that at-tack on certain forms of wickedness is approval of their opposites. To attack pride is to commend humility.

The satirist is an artist who is constantly giving himself away, con-stantly exposing his dearest principles and his utopian wishes. Whether to avoid involvement or whatever, satirists sometimes efface themselves through the use of irony or *dramatis personae*. But even in ironic satire the polarities remain; it is simply harder to get at the author's purposes and meanings. In Swift's ironic satire regularly appear little moments of discovery, epiphanies, which clarify the tendency of the art. A clear instance of this is in the *Modest Proposal,* in the sentences which begin: ". . . let no man talk to me of other Expedients." The *Argument against Abolishing Christianity* seems to be a shiftier irony. But there are clues enough; for example, in the pun which is slipped into the argument that parsons are useful to society since they serve as the butt of jokes by wits, "who may safely rail on, without danger to their *persons.*"

The satirist uses a *persona,* usually, to let the opposition condemn

itself. The putative author of *A Tale of a Tub* represents by his own
pretensions modern writers. His folly reflects on that which he represents, and it has never been a secret, even if "hidden" in irony, that
Swift sided with the ancients, the conservatives, the humanists, against
the trends of the modern world.

Today a general feeling exists that satirists, as do other artists, create
for self-relief, self-expression, or high aesthetic ineffables—but never for
the persuasive expression of moral principles. The true artist, we know
today, is above the polarities of right and wrong in which the satirist is
sometimes assumed to be involved. Attributing such amoral objectivity
to satire clashes, however, with the self-interpretation of satirists, at least
through Swift's day.

Indeed, the trouble which Swift creates for critics is that he forces
them to consider moral issues, to react to his "values." The skill with
which he controls the reader's moral sensibility is the heart of his
aesthetic. The brilliance of the destructive technique, juxtaposing vices
and objects of disgust, sometimes blinds the reader to the affirmative
elements of his satire, in which what Swift approves receives sympathetic
depiction.

In *Gulliver's Travels* Swift makes full use of the two time-honored
satiric techniques, which I shall term the destructive and the affirmative.
The complicating factor is Gulliver's role in the various patterns. As the
pattern changes from book to book, and Gulliver's function with it, the
reader errs in seeking a single omnipresent technique. One can not find
in Gulliver a character such as one finds, says, in an ordinary novel.
In the complex scheme of the book Gulliver is the flexible vehicle of the
satire—at one time the representative of virtue, at another the embodiment of vice; sometimes wise, sometimes foolish. In the following
analyses of the *Travels* I have tried to understand the ethical antitheses
of each part and to place these antitheses in the formal structure of the
plot which Swift devised in each voyage.

I

GULLIVER'S MORAL STATURE

On his first voyage Gulliver's nature proves to be as good, in comparison with that of the Lilliputians, as his body is large. Gulliver's
merits reveal themselves from the time of his first encounter with the
little men, who appear at first in a fairly advantageous light: they bind
the sleeping Gulliver, who awakens unable to move; and when he
struggles to get loose they subdue him with volleys of tiny arrows. He

makes signs that he is hungry and receives a generous breakfast, generous considering the size of the Lilliputians:

> I confess I was often tempted, while they were passing backwards and
> forwards on my Body [as they carried food to his mouth], to seize Forty
> or Fifty of the first that came in my Reach, and dash them against the
> Ground. But the Remembrance of what I had felt [from their arrows],
> which probably might not be the worst they could do; and the Promise
> of Honour I made them, for so I interpreted my submissive Behaviour,
> soon drove out those Imaginations. Besides, I now considered my self
> as bound by the Laws of Hospitality to a People who had treated me
> with so much Expence and Magnificence. (I, i, 5)[1]

From the first, Gulliver is grateful for the kindness that he receives, even
from creatures far inferior, at least in strength. Much later, even after
the Emperor of Lilliput and his council decide to punish Gulliver for
his well-intentioned and beneficent actions, Gulliver refuses to stoop to
any base designs:

> Once I was strongly bent upon Resistance: For while I had Liberty,
> the whole Strength of that Empire could hardly subdue me, and I might
> easily with Stones pelt the Metropolis to Pieces: But I soon rejected
> that Project with Horror, by remembering the Oath I had made to the
> Emperor [swearing peace with him], the Favours I received from him,
> and the high Title of Nardac he conferred upon me. Neither had I so
> soon learned the Gratitude of Courtiers, to persuade myself that his
> Majesty's present Severities acquitted me of all past Obligations. (I, vii,
> 22)

Not only as gratitude, which Swift thought a virtue,[2] but also as mercy
and generosity, does Gulliver's benevolence come to light: chained to
his quarters (an abandoned, defiled church), Gulliver becomes a center
of attention, and must be guarded:

> . . . to prevent the Impertinence, and probably the Malice of the Rabble,
> who were very impatient to croud about me as near as they durst; and
> some of them had the Impudence to shoot their Arrows at me as I sate
> on the Ground by the Door of my House; whereof one very narrowly
> missed my left Eye. But the Colonel ordered six of the Ringleaders to
> be seized, and thought no Punishment so proper as to deliver them
> bound into my Hands, which some of his Soldiers accordingly did, push-
> ing them forwards with the But-ends of their Pikes into my Reach: I
> took them all in my right Hand, put five of them into my Coat-pocket;
> as to the sixth, I made a Countenance as if I would eat him alive. The
> poor Man squalled terribly, and the Colonel and his officers were in

---

[1] All citations to *Gulliver's Travels* are made by giving book, chapter, and paragraph numbers. I quote from PW, XI.
[2] See his strictures on ingratitude, PW, VIII, 6, 11–12; C, 11, 26–27, 33–35, J, I,
88, 334.

much Pain, especially when they saw me take out my Penknife: But I
soon put them out of Fear; for, looking mildly, and immediately cutting the Strings he was bound with, I set him gently on the Ground,
and away he ran. I treated the rest in the same Manner, taking them
one by one out of my Pocket; and I observed, both the Soldiers and
People were highly obliged at this Mark of my Clemency, which was
represented very much to my Advantage at Court. (I, ii, 3)

So favorable was the impression that the Emperor issued a commission
"obliging all the Villages nine hundred Yards round the City" to furnish
the victuals necessary for Gulliver's sustenance (I, ii, 6). Gradually his
"Gentleness and good Behaviour" win him the trust of the natives, who
"came by Degrees to be less apprehensive of any Danger from me. . . .
And at last the Boys and Girls would venture to come and play at Hide
and Seek in my Hair" (I, iii, 1).

Gulliver's behavior in Lilliput, even his bloodless victory over the
Blefuscun fleet, is all docility, gentleness, and modesty: he returns with
the enemy fleet in tow, shouting to the tiny prince, "Long live the most
puissant Emperor of Lilliput!":

> His Majesty desired I would take some other Opportunity of bring-
> ing all the rest of his Enemy's Ships into his Ports. And so unmeasurable
> is the Ambition of Princes, that he seemed to think of nothing less than
> reducing the whole Empire of Blefuscu into a Province, and governing
> it by a Viceroy; of destroying the Big-Endian Exiles, and compelling
> that People to break the smaller End of their Eggs; by which he would
> remain sole Monarch of the whole World. But I endeavoured to divert
> him from this Design, by many Arguments drawn from the Topicks of
> Policy as well as Justice: And I plainly protested that I would never be
> an Instrument of bringing a free and brave People into Slavery. (I,
> v, 4)

The Emperor's ambition is thrown into relief by the innocence, the
generosity, the magnanimity of Gulliver's attitude: like the most idealistic of the Roman republicans,[3] or the Humanists, Gulliver will not use
his power in a bad cause. The ambassadors sent from Blefuscu to sue for
peace have the good sense to pay Gulliver "many Compliments" on his
"Valour and Generosity" (I, v, 6) in opposing the Lilliputian Emperor's ambitions.

At times in Book I, Gulliver represents Swift's idea of magnanimity
(appropriately in a correspondingly large body): great talents em-

---

[3] Love of liberty is an important subtheme of the book and is a counterpart to the
republicanism of the third voyage. On war, cf. Cicero, *De Officiis*, I, xi: "The only
excuse, therefore, for going to war is that we may live in peace unharmed," tr.
Walter Miller (London: Heinemann, 1928).

ployed for public good, of such integrity as to be above any base action, and humane, generous, innocent, and modest.[4] He seems a well-intentioned young hero, say a Telemachus, who goodheartedly and awkwardly discovers the meanness of the men who make up his world. His adventures in Lilliput form the initiation of a rather idealistic young man who tries to get along in a world which he is later shocked to understand. That he has a different character in the second voyage is evident enough if we compare Gulliver's cold-blooded attempt to give the Brobdingnag king the secret of gunpowder with Gulliver's friendly warning to the Emperor of Lilliput:

> I delivered up both my Pistols . . . and then my Pouch of Powder and Bullets; begging him that the former might be kept from Fire; for it would kindle with the smallest Spark, and blow up his Imperial Palace into the Air. (I, ii, 10)

His innocence is almost naïveté; it seems to me the naïveté of a young idealist: he is impressed by the bravery and the technical skill of the Lilliputians (I, i, 7; ii, 6). To the sophisticated reader Gulliver must seem an *ingénu*. Yet a rare *ingénu* he is! Of gigantic comparative strength, he ingenuously wonders at physical distinctions among the little men: the Emperor, he observes, "is taller by almost the Breadth of my Nail, than any of his Court; which alone is enough to strike an Awe into the Beholders" (I, ii, 3). Gulliver's modesty is almost so excessive as to be craven: the Lilliputians chain him like a dog, and Gulliver becomes a friendly animal, an affable freak, who entertains the populace or the court with his appetite or his handkerchief.[5] Gulliver prostrates himself before the emperors of Blefuscu and Lilliput, yet dares to tell the latter that he will not help "force the Consciences, or destroy the Liberties and Lives of an innocent People" (I, vii, 9).

With his humanistic attitude toward war, Gulliver is willing to fight to defend the Emperor and his country against invaders; but he will not pursue the war simply for the glory to be got at the cost of enslaving a free people. The parallel to the Tory attitude toward Marlborough's continental campaigns against France is clear; the Tories were the "Lovers of Peace," Swift believed (PW, VII, 3, 26).[6]

Since Gulliver is given a good character in Lilliput, it is said that he represents not just Swift's ethical preferences, but some actual persons

[4] See Chapter 4.
[5] Gulliver is mettlesome enough, however, to want his freedom and to dislike the articles of peace, which he finds too "servile."
[6] Swift himself thought a reader need not be aware of the historical allegory to understand his book: see C, III, 407.

he admired—either Harley, or St. John, or both.[7] In view of Gulliver's military valor, his attitude toward peace, and his modesty, Ormonde (whom Swift liked) is also a good guess, if we consider the following character, which Swift gave him:

> . . . the Attainder of the Duke of Ormonde . . . looks like a Dream, to those who consider the Nobleness of his Birth, the great Merits of his Ancestors and his own, his long unspotted Loyalty; his Affability, Generosity, and Sweetness of Nature. I knew him long and well; and excepting the Frailtyes of his Youth, which had been for some Years over, and that easyness of Temper which did sometimes lead him to follow the Judgment of those who had by many degrees less Understanding than himself; I have not conversed with a more faultless Person; of great Justice and Charity, a true sense of Religion without Ostentation; of undoubted Valour, throwly skilled in his Trade as a Souldier; a quick and ready Apprehension, with a good Share of Understanding, and a generall Knowledge in Men and History, although under some Disadvantage by an invincible Modesty, which however could not but render him yet more amiable to those who had the Honour and Happiness of being throwly acquainted with Him. (PW, VIII, 132–133)

Others besides Swift comment on the aspects of Ormonde's character which resemble Gulliver's: magnanimity, generosity, and integrity.[8] One trait ascribed to Gulliver in Part I hardly has a parallel in Oxford or Bolingbroke—his modesty—whereas Swift stresses exactly that in his praise of Ormonde.

But several other activities of Ormonde's suggest that Swift modeled Gulliver on the Duke in the first voyage. In 1712, since surreptitious peace negotiations between the French and English were underway, Ormande was ordered not to attack. Since the orders were secret, he could give no satisfactory reasons for his inaction to England's allies, and consequently felt dishonored and humiliated—as did Gulliver in swearing to the articles of peace, which were not as honorable as he might have wished. Further, we know from the *Journal to Stella* that Ormonde was instrumental in trying to put out a fire on one occasion:

> . . . it was my poor Brother Sr Wm Windham's house was burnt; and . . . 2 maids leaping out of an upper room to avoyd the Fire, both fell on their Heads; one of them upon the Iron Spikes before the door; and both lay dead in the Streets; it is supposed to have been some Carelessness of one or both those Maids. The D. of Ormd was there, helping to put out the Fire. (J, II, 502)

---

[7] Charles Firth, "The Political Significance of *Gulliver's Travels,*" *Essays Historical and Literary* (Oxford: Clarendon, 1938), pp. 219–220.

[8] See, for example, John Lodge, *The Peerage of Ireland*, rev. Mervyn Archdall (Dublin: J. Moore, 1789). IV, n. 62; and A. W. W[ard]., "James Butler," *DNB*.

Also, in action against the Spanish, Ormonde captured and destroyed a large portion of the enemy's fleet; this action Swift recalled in writing a few lines in defense of the Duke of Ormonde, accused by the Whigs of treason:

> . . . he no more conceived himself to be acting high Treason than he did when he was wounded and a Prisoner at Landen for his Sovereign King William: or when he took and burned the Enemyes Fleet at Vigo. (PW, VIII, 133)

And, last, Gulliver's title in Lilliput was that of Nardac, "which is the highest Title of Honour among them"—and the equivalent of Duke in England.

If Gulliver resembles in important facets the magnanimous men whom Swift admired, one action of his becomes a hieroglyph of the fate of the too highly gifted public servant. Swift criticized, while he admired, the great men of affairs who sought to achieve some public good by means of an uncommon or daring policy (even as they labored under the burden of a general envy of their superiority). The "Infelicity" of such magnanimous statesmen (as Themistocles, Aristides, Scipio, Sir Walter Raleigh, Bacon, Clarendon, Strafford, Laud, Oxford, and Bolingbroke), their fall from power or their disgrace, Swift believed "to have been caused by their Neglect of common Forms, together with the Contempt of little Helps, and little Hindrances; which is made by Hobbes the Definition of Magnanimity; And the Contempt, as it certainly displeases the People in generall, so it giveth Offence to all with whom such Ministers have to deal" (PW, VIII, 138–139).[9]

Consider then Gulliver, like one of Swift's magnanimous men, in a moment of great exigency: the palace of Lilliput has caught fire. With little helps, buckets "about the Size of a large Thimble," which are almost little hindrances because they do "little Good," Gulliver tries to put out the fire:

> The Case seemed wholly desperate and deplorable; and this magnificent Palace would have infallibly been burnt down to the Ground, if, by a Presence of Mind, unusual to me, I had not suddenly thought of an Expedient. I had the Evening before drank plentifully of a most delicious Wine . . . which is very diuretick. By the luckiest Chance in the World, I had not discharged myself of any Part of it. . . . which I voided in such a Quantity, and applied so well to the proper Places, that in three Minutes the Fire was wholly extinguished; and the rest of that noble Pile, which had cost so many Ages in erecting, preserved from Destruction. (I, v, 9)

[9] See also PW, XIII, 38–39; C, III, 41–42.

Gulliver's adventures are an allegory of the fate of the magnanimous, modest, good-natured, and benevolent public servant, whose good actions (perhaps a little out of common forms) result in punishment by the petty, ungrateful, unjust, and vicious men whom he helps.

II

THE PETTY VICIOUSNESS OF THE LILLIPUTIANS

Gulliver rendered two great services to the Emperor of Lilliput: he destroyed the enemy fleet which threatened Lilliput, and he extinguished the fire and preserved at least parts of the palace. But in both instances Gulliver was to suffer by the ingratitude and injustice of courts. In the first, Gulliver's republicanism and love of liberty prevented his acquiescing in the Emperor's military ambitions:

> And from this Time began an Intrigue between his Majesty, and a Junta of Ministers maliciously bent against me, which . . . had like to have ended in my utter Destruction. Of so little Weight are the greatest Services to Princes, when put into the Balance with a Refusal to gratify their Passions. (I, v, 5)

In the instance of the fire, just as in the preliminary arrangements for the Peace of Utrecht,[10] a great good was achieved in not so honorable or usual a manner:

> And I was privately assured, that the Empress conceiving the greatest Abhorrence of what I had done, removed to the most distant Side of the Court, firmly resolved that those Buildings should never be repaired for her Use; and, in the Presence of her chief Confidents, could not forbear vowing Revenge. (I, v, 10)

Gulliver's reward, then, for two benefactions is death for treason, as outlined in the articles of impeachment drawn up by the Emperor and his ministers in secret (I, vii, 6 ff.). Gulliver's "friend," Reldresal, has argued with the ministers for mercy, and suggests that the crinimal be only blinded; finally, it is resolved that the official published punishment is to be blinding, while the secret intention is to starve him after he is blinded: "Thus by the great Friendship of the Secretary [Reldresal], the whole Affair was compromised" (I, vii, 18). Their injustice is as great as their ingratitude; but justice is a thing unknown in that court, where preferences go not to virtue, but "Dexterity" or nimbleness: offices and honors are "earned" by cutting capers on tight ropes or in

---

[10] See A. E. Case, *Four Essays on "Gulliver's Travels"* (Princeton: Princeton University Press, 1945), pp. 74 ff.

leaping over and creeping under a baton held by the Emperor (I, iii, 2–4).

The courtiers' gymnastics, directed by the Emperor for his pleasure and diversion, are perhaps a spoof at Hobbes' insistence that the justice of the subject or citizen consists of his compliance with the will of the sovereign, however capricious that will and however much contrary to the best interests of the citizen. Hobbes' third law of nature is that one must keep his contract with the ruler, to whom one owes complete obedience.[11] Also, as noted earlier, Hobbes felt that no subject of worth could claim that something is due to him by justice, that the ruler has a duty to reward merit. Hobbes seems to have seen the function of the ruler as necessarily punitive; the ruler is thus bound to punish bad actions, such as theft or murder, but is not required to reward good actions. Quite different is the Lilliputian ideal of justice (which the courtiers do not follow):

> And these People thought it a prodigious Defect of Policy among us, when I told them that our Laws were enforced only by Penalties, without Mention of Reward. It is upon this account that the Image of Justice, in their Courts of Judicature, is formed with six Eyes, two before, as many behind, and on each Side one, to signify Circumspection; with a Bag of Gold open in her right Hand, and a Sword sheathed in her left, to shew she is more disposed to reward than to punish. (I, vi, 6)

One of Swift's dearest principles was that men of worth must be rewarded by those in power.

The Lilliputians are remarkable for their cruelty: Skyresh Bolgolam takes great pleasure in forcing "Articles and Conditions" upon Gulliver before he is set free (I, iii, 8); the Emperor is anxious to conquer Blefuscu and thereby "to destroy and put to death not only all the Big-Endian Exiles [his own people], but likewise all the People of that Empire, who would not immediately forsake the Big-Endian Heresy" (I, vii, 9); the Emperor's advisors are resourceful and zestful in imagining ways to murder their benefactor, Gulliver; Reldresal stands by his friend and asks that he *only* be blinded. Similar viciousness they direct against each other, for in politics there are "Animosities" over the great issue of the height of one's heels; and in religion the bitterest controversy has raged over which end of the egg is to be cracked first, according to their bible. The issues between the High-Heels and Low-Heels, and the Big-Endians and Little-Endians have generated bloody persecutions and the protracted war between Lilliput and Blefuscu (I, iv). By means of

---

[11] *Leviathan*, XV, (93); see also XVIII (115), XXI (139), and XXVI (173).

such symbols as the breaking of eggs and the height of heels, Swift not only makes the satirical point that religious and political questions are usually per se inconsequential, but also reveals that quarrels over trifles actually result from contentious, litigious viciousness.

As ludicrous as the disparity between such trifling issues and the wars they become is the diminutive stature of the Lilliputians, when compared to their pride or vanity; the Emperor of this little people is known as the

> Delight and Terror of the Universe, whose Dominions extend five Thousand Blustrugs, (above twelve Miles in Circumference) to the Extremities of the Globe: Monarch of all Monarchs: Taller than the Sons of Men; whose Feet press down to the Center, and whose Head strikes against the Sun. (I, iii, 9)

Gulliver's presence accentuates the folly of such pretensions.

III

Reversible Vehicles

A central feature of Swift's technique as a satirist is a quirk, a relish for exploiting all the humor latent in a character or situation.[12] Gulliver, in all his voyages, is sometimes foolish, sometimes wise (but generally in one voyage tending to be primarily one or the other). In Lilliput he is generally admirable and virtuous, although at times he has faults enough.[13] He is foolishly vain as he plays the ladies' man in exculpating one of the tiny women of criminal conversation with him (I, vi. 22). And when her husband, the Lord Treasurer, favors Gulliver with a little disdain:

> . . . I had the Honour [Gulliver assures the reader] to be a Nardac, which the Treasurer himself is not; for all World knows he is only a Clumglum, a Title inferior by one Degree, as that of a Marquess is to a Duke in England. (I, vi, 22)

If we assume that Gulliver in Lilliput at least recalls the Harley-St. John ministry, Gulliver's vainglory is then a reflection on St. John's behavior after the Guiscard affair: Harley got all the glory and became an earl, whereas St. John was mortified at being made only a viscount. Also, the

---

[12] See R. S. Crane, "The Rationale of the Fourth Voyage," *Gulliver's Travels* (text and critical essays), ed. R. A. Greenberg (New York: W. W. Norton, 1961), p. 305.

[13] Swift liked to intermix praise and dispraise: he paid the highest compliments to Arbuthnot and added, ". . . but alas! he has a sort of slouch in his walk" (C, III, 278).

munificence which the diet of Gulliver necessitates is reminiscent of Marlborough's magnificent scale of life, which (Swift felt) was a heavy drain on the English treasury. Noteworthy, too, is that Gulliver, like Marlborough, was invincible. But Ormonde was another extragavant liver, as Swift remarked to Stella in speaking of the visit of a French ambassador, who was "a fine Gentleman, something like the D. Ormd, and just such an expensive man" (J, II, 596).

The Lilliputians themselves are not all bad: Gulliver admires their courage and resourcefulness; and, like Ebenezor Elliston, Gulliver found one honest man in that country, "a considerable Person at Court," who tells Gulliver of the secret proceedings of the Emperor and the junta against him; this man is the only truly grateful one in Lilliput: he brings Gulliver the timely warning "out of Gratitude" for past favors which Gulliver had rendered him (I, vii, 3–7). The pattern is the usual one in Swift's survey of the ways of the world: there is much evil and, surprisingly, a little genuine good.

The central paradox of Book I is that this land of vicious little people should be described, in Chapter VI, as a kind of utopia. Critics have seized on this incongruity as proof that Swift worked up the book from an earlier sketch, of a mainly utopian country, and that the retainment of the earlier utopian elements is a serious flaw in the fabric of the book. Swift himself, it is argued, was aware of his faulty architectonics and hit upon an inadequate remedy:[14] Gulliver tries to explain the contradiction, in the midst of a discussion of the excellences of Lilliput:

> In relating these and the following Laws, I would only be understood to mean the original Institutions, and not the most scandalous Corruptions into which these People are fallen by the degenerate Nature of Man. (I, vi, 9)

But, if Swift saw the fault, was it not laziness or folly to fail to rewrite the voyage or to make a few changes in Chapter VI? Was Swift such a dull or clumsy writer?

However, any objection to the structure of Book I must grow out of an examination of that structure, and not merely out of an apparent contradiction (to which the author himself calls attention). Chapter VI has a crucial position in the action of the first voyage, and forms, in fact, a kind of interlude between Gulliver's two benevolent actions (conquering the fleet and extinguishing the fire) and his discovery of the "reward" which the Emperor has in store for him and of the extent to

---

[14] E.g., see Ricardo Quintana, *The Mind and Art of Jonathan Swift* (London: Oxford University Press, 1953), p. 309.

which Lilliputian ingratitude, injustice, and cruelty could go, in the
form of fraudulent articles of impeachment based on the evidence of
false witnesses.[15]

The utopian laws and institutions which Gulliver seems incongruously
to pause to consider are not unconnected with this action (I, vi, 4–15):

[1]   The first . . . relateth to Informers. All Crimes against the State,
are punished here with the utmost Severity; but if the Person accused
make his Innocence plainly to appear upon his Tryal, the Accuser is
immediately put to an ignominious Death.

[2]   They look upon Fraud as a greater Crime than Theft, and therefore seldom fail to punish it with Death: For they alledge . . . Honesty
hath no Fence against superior Cunning.

[3]   [Whoever can prove he has] strictly observed the Laws of his Country for Seventy-three Moons [is rewarded with money and a title].

[4]   In chusing Persons of all Employments, they have more Regard to
good Morals than to great Abilities . . . they suppose Truth, Justice,
Temperance, and the like, to be in every Man's Power . . . *the Mistakes
committed by Ignorance in a virtuous Disposition,* would never be of
such fatal Consequence to the Publick Weal, as the Practices of a Man,
whose Inclinations led him to be corrupt, and had great Abilities to manage, to multiply, and defend his Corruptions (italics mine).

[5]   In like Manner, the Disbelief of a Divine Providence renders a
Man uncapable of holding any publick Station.

[6]   Ingratitude is among them a capital Crime . . . For they reason
thus; that whoever makes ill Returns to his Benefactor, must needs be
a common Enemy to the rest of Mankind, from whom he hath received
no Obligation; and therefore such a Man is not fit to live.

[7]   . . . Parents are the last of all others to be trusted with the Education of their own Children [who are therefore educated in state nurseries
and there] bred up in the Principles of Honour, Justice, Courage, Modesty, Clemency, Religion, and Love of their Country [No pampering
or spoiling is allowed. Girls are educated to be as courageous and sensible as boys and to] despise all personal Ornaments beyond Decency
and Cleanliness.[16]

In Chapter VII, where Gulliver learns the worst about the Lilliputians, he comments on the disparity between principles and practice:
nothing terrifies Lilliputians, he notes, more than "Encomiums on his
Majesty's Mercy; because it was observed, that the more these Praises
were enlarged and insisted on, the more inhuman was the Punishment,
and the Sufferer more innocent" (I, vii, 22). Chapter VI, the utopian
chapter, furnishes the entire book with the same irony: in Lilliput,

[15] See Chapter 2.
[16] I omit a few laws and customs.

where false informing, fraud, and ingratitude are capital crimes, where all public servants are selected for their good morals and must believe in God, where every child is taught justice and clemency—here it is that the Emperor and the highest public officers violate nearly all the basic laws and deny their own education and principles in their illegal proceeding against Gulliver. There is no flaw or contradiction in the structure of the book; rather there is a flaw or contradiction in the actions of men, who proceed with inhumanity against their own principles. A technique of satire is not a defect of composition.

"A Voyage to Lilliput" reveals an unfortunate truth about human behavior. The satirist is not utopian, but the ordinary members of society are, for they hold up principles as good while ignoring them. The concept of what is best is given lip service by ordinary men, who thus admit the ideal even as they fail to follow it. The satirist, unpleasant human type, makes a point of disclosing the discrepancy in the utopian pretensions of ordinary life and the everyday behavior of men with such pretensions. The satirist is utopian only in wishing that the better, or utopian, inclinations of society might prevail.

CHAPTER 7

Gulliver Glorioso

In the first part of the *Travels* the structure of the plot on the level of action must be defined with reference to the pattern of Gulliver's bad fortune of shipwreck and capture, his good fortune of becoming a free man and military hero, his bad fortune of being envied and betrayed, and his final good fortune of escape to his homeland. On this framework of action Swift placed a fabric of moral contrast: between the benevolence of Gulliver and the cruelty of the Lilliputians, between Lilliputian "values" and Lilliputian practice.

Likewise, in the second voyage we find a conventional plot involving capture and escape, but here the question is no longer mainly whether the hero will suffer good or bad fortune. That is, the story develops little tension as to Gulliver's personal safety, although he is often in danger. What is constantly threatened is Gulliver's dignity, his self-respect, his pride. Early in the story, as the giant reapers come closer and closer to Gulliver, hidden in a field of grain, a few thoughts run through his mind:

> I reflected what a Mortification it must prove to me to appear as inconsiderable in this Nation, as one single Lilliputian would be among us. But, this I conceived was to be the least of my Misfortunes: For, as human Creatures are observed to be more Savage and cruel in Proportion to their Bulk; what could I expect but to be a Morsel in the Mouth of the first among these enormous Barbarians who should happen to seize me? (II, i, 5)

The ironic untruth of these two reflections, that experiences in Brobdingnag will mortify him or his pride and that the natives will prove as cruel and vicious as large, controls the structure of Part II—the one on the level of action, the other on the level of ethics. The plot embodies the first in the erratic career of Gulliver's pride, which he continually bolsters, only to have it again deflated. On the second level the increasingly dominant pattern is the contrast between Gulliver (his civilization) and the giant king. These two levels are distinct, of course, only in analysis, for Swift contrived to have both build to a common point of climax.

I
IRREPRESSIBLE PRIDE

The almost obtrusive comic pattern in Part II is the alternation of Gulliver's heroic pretensions and humiliating experiences. His size in itself should have induced modesty; and his earliest experiences are not flattering. A reaper regards him as "a small dangerous Animal"; a farmer puts him on all fours, like a small animal; the farmer's wife, at the sight of Gulliver, "screamed and ran back as Women in England do at the Sight of a Toad or a Spider" (II, i, 6–8).

But Gulliver, betraying not one whit of chagrin, feels that the King of England would have had to suffer the same, under similar circumstances (II, ii, 2). Thus, the pattern establishes itself: humiliation, reasserted pride. In reasserting his pride Gulliver speaks of his actions in heroic style—which to the reader is mock-heroic: he tells us of facing an elephantine cat which is afraid of him, of courageously fighting two rats, of performing assorted foolish stunts "ten Times a Day to the Wonder and Satisfaction of all People" (II, i, 10, 14; ii, 8).

Like many proud men, Gulliver winds up at court, thanks (he says) to his gallantries toward the Queen and the report from her ladies concerning Gulliver's "Beauty, Behaviour, and good Sense." The Queen buys Gulliver at what he considers a bargain price: ". . . hardly so great a Sum as a Thousand Guineas would be in England." Thanks, too, to Gulliver's timely request and credit with the Queen, Glumdalclitch, the farmer's daughter, is "preferred" at Court—that is, allowed to enter the Queen's service as Gulliver's nurse. Gulliver complains to the Queen, as soon as he is bought, that the work enforced on him by the farmer's greed "was laborious enough to kill an Animal of ten Times" his strength: that is, of the strength of a Brobdingnagian! (II, iii, 1–2).

The King (Gulliver tells us) directed that "particular Care" be taken of him; and the Queen becomes so fond of Gulliver's company "that she could not dine without" him (II, iii, 7–8). The tiny Gulliver becomes a "Favourite" (so he says) of this sixty-foot King and sits, during meals, at the King's "left Hand *before one of the* Salt-sellers" (italics mine). He and the King often converse about European politics, wars, sects, parties: on one occasion the King strokes him as one would a favorite cat and observes "how contemptible a Thing [is] human Grandeur, which could be mimicked by such diminutive Insects" as Gulliver (II, iii, 9).

But *superbia vincit omnia,* as Gulliver reveals in telling of the Queen's ordering a new, smaller box to be made for his convenience in traveling: this box is to be carried by "some grave trusty Servant in whom I could confide, whether I attended the King and Queen in their Progresses, or were disposed to see the Gardens, or pay a Visit to some great Lady or Minister of State in the Court . . . For I soon began to be known and esteemed among the greatest Officers." And Gulliver is proud enough to add, in false modesty: "I suppose more upon Account of their Majesty's Favour, than any Merit of my own" (II, iv, 5).

After this high point of pride and pretense Gulliver, in Chapter V, undergoes some terribly humiliating experiences: he is almost killed by dwarf-apples shaken from a tree, bruised by a hailstorm, retrieved by a dog ("But, the Thing was hushed up, and never known at Court"), dirtied by a fall into a molehill (whereupon he "coined some Lye not worth remembering, to excuse my self for spoiling my Cloaths"). He breaks his shin against a snail shell; the maids of honor pester him with various naughty "Tricks"; a frog invades and beslimes his boat; a monkey takes him to be its baby, carries him to the top of the castle, and force feeds him with food stored in its jaws. The last adventure puts the whole "Quarter of the Palace . . . in an Uproar," Gulliver affirms; and the King rallies Gulliver for his fright on the roof top, while Gulliver plays a sad Falstaff in asserting his courage. But Gulliver's vainglory receives its greatest setback at the end of Chapter V: on an outing with Glumdalclitch, Gulliver finds:

> . . . a Cow-dung in the Path, and I must needs try my Activity by attempting to leap over it. I took a Run, but unfortunately jumped short, and found my self just in the Middle up to my Knees. I waded through with some Difficulty, and one of the Footmen wiped me as clean as he could with his Handkerchief; for I was filthily bemired . . . the Queen was soon informed of what had passed, and the Footmen spread it about the Court; so that all the Mirth, for some Days, was at my Expence.

But Gulliver must reassert his dignity—by showing his skill in "fine" workmanship and by playing a jig on a giant spinet for the court. At this point Gulliver himself takes on the responsibility of representing Europe against the contempt in which the King holds it; and Gulliver ambitiously believes that he will "live to do his Majesty some signal Service" (II, vi, 5). The King then asks for an exact account of the English government, and gets from Gulliver a romanticized, idealized picture of justice and public spirit. From contradictions in Gulliver's account and in his answers to a hundred perspicacious questions, the King decides that there is no justice, public spirit, or virtue of any kind in England; and Gulliver, a representative of such a society, stands condemned as a member of "the most pernicious Race of little odious Vermin that

Nature ever suffered to crawl upon the Surface of the Earth" (II, vi, 18).

And yet Gulliver persists. He thinks that "it would be hard indeed, if so remote a Prince's Notions of Virtue and Vice were to be offered as a Standard for all Mankind" (II, vii, 2). He will still try to do the King some great service: he tells him about gunpowder, an invention unknown to the Brobdingnagians; he outlines the wonderful destructiveness that dwells on the bloody carnage it produces:

> The King was struck with Horror at the Description I had given of those terrible Engines, and the Proposal I had made. He was amazed how so impotent and groveling an Insect as I (these were his Expressions) could entertain such inhuman Ideas, and in so familiar a Manner as to appear wholly unmoved at all the Scenes of Blood and Desolation, which I had painted as the common Effects of those destructive Machines; whereof he said, some evil Genius, Enemy to Mankind, must have been the first Contriver. As for himself, he protested, that although few Things delighted him so much as new Discoveries in Art or in Nature; yet he would rather lose Half his Kingdom than be privy to such a Secret; which he commanded me, as I valued my Life, never to mention any more. (II, vii, 4)

That is Gulliver's and Europe's lowest point: he and it stand condemned as petty, unjust, vicious, and inhuman.

Gulliver still prattles of recovering his liberty and of the "Dignity of human Kind" (II, viii, 1); and, through no virtue of his own, he escapes: a giant eagle carries his box out to sea and drops it, perhaps in a fight with two others. The honest captain who rescues Gulliver rallies him a little on his difficulties in readjusting to the pigmy world of ordinary people; and he jokes about Gulliver's fall to the sea. And "the Comparison of Phaeton was so obvious, that he could not forbear applying it, although I did not much admire the Conceit" (II, viii, 13). Phaeton's story is the classic one of the little man who tries, out of vanity or pride, to do too big a job: to drive his father's chariot. The captain (that is, Swift) thus hit upon the perfect vehicle to represent the career of Gulliver in Brobdingnag, except that Gulliver's pride goes before a score of falls, and continues after them.

Gulliver's life in Brobdingnag is a parody of the adventures of storybook heroes. Instead, however, of escaping from one danger to another in a sequence which leads to the greatest danger of all at the climax of the story, Gulliver "heroically" sustains his false sense of dignity through one danger after another. Without the King as foil, Gulliver of Part II could be construed as an archetype of the twentieth-century antihero, a Willy Loman, who elicits our queasy sympathy. But in Swift's satire

Gulliver Glorioso has no such cozy place; representative of the most unflagging and worst of human failings—pride—Gulliver is the obverse of Everyman or Bunyan's Christian, for the question for him is not whether he will fall into dangers which lead to the destruction of his soul, but, comically, whether he will suffer disaster to enlarge his soul. Gulliver, of course, in Part II, is incapable of enlargement.

II
THE HEROIC IDEAL

The King and Gulliver present the moral polarities of Part II, Gulliver insisting on being the spokesman for England (and Europe). The brilliant technique of Chapter VI, the chapter in which the King rips off the veneer of Gulliver's panegyric, has attracted the praise of critics, who therefore, perhaps, do not devote sufficient attention to the exact nature of the antagonism of principles in the conversation. In view of the increasing interest in Swift's technique—that is, the use of masks— perhaps Swiftians need to remember the Bee's advice to the Spider: ". . . consider Duration *and matter,* as well as method and Art" (PW, I, 149; italics mine).

Much of the art in the construction of the scene in Chapter VI results from the peculiar substance of Gulliver's speech in praise of England. His praise implies the classical understanding of justice: the public honors should be the reward of virtue; that the just, the virtuous, should rule; that each man should mind his proper business.[1] The irony of Gulliver's praise of the House of Lords is that he himself implies the argument against hereditary nobility; according to strict justice, the truly noble should rule, rather than those who gain such a right by accident of birth:

> I described that extraordinary Care always taken of their Education in Arts and Arms, to qualify them for being Counsellors born to the King and Kingdom . . . to be Champions always ready for the Defence of their Prince and Country by their Valour, Conduct and Fidelity .That these were the Ornament and Bulwark of the Kingdom; worthy Followers of their most renowned Ancestors, whose Honour had been the Reward of their Virtue; from which their Posterity were never once known to degenerate. (II, vi, 7)

Similarly, Gulliver praises the bishops of England as "deservedly distinguished by the Sanctity of their Lives, and the Depth of their Erudition." And the members of the House of Commons (according to Gulliver) "were all principal Gentlemen, freely picked and culled out

[1] For example, cf. Aristotle, *Nicomachean Ethics,* V, iii.

by the People themselves, for their great Abilities, and Love of their
Country, to represent the Wisdom of the whole Nation" (II, vi, 7–8).

The King however separates fact from fiction, vices from panegyric.
He asks how the nobility are educated; how they spend their time; how
new peers are selected; whether private interests predominate over public in any selections; whether the lords know the laws of the land;
whether they are truly public spirited or dominated by selfish motives.
He wonders whether those who become bishops are not "Compliers with
the Times . . . or slavish prostitute Chaplains to some Nobleman" before
their advancement (II, vi, 11).

The King is puzzled by the assiduity of the commoners in standing for
parliament:

> . . . without any Salary or Pension: Because this appeared such an ex-
> alted Strain of Virtue and publick Spirit, that his Majesty seemed to
> doubt it might possibly not be always sincere: And he desired to know,
> whether such zealous Gentlemen could have any Views of refunding
> themselves for the Charges and Trouble they were at, by sacrificing the
> publick Good to the Designs of a weak and vicious Prince, in Conjunc-
> tion with a corrupted Ministry. (II, vi, 12)

Adumbrated here is another element in the classical understanding of
justice, that justice is rule for the common good. Orrery observed that
"Swift's principle of government seems to have been founded upon that
excellent motto, *Salus populi suprema est lex.*"[2]

The King concludes that Gulliver's panegyric finally shows that there
is no justice, no rule for the public good, no virtue, no public spirit to
be found in England:

> You have clearly proved that Ignorance, Idleness, and Vice are the
> proper Ingredients for qualifying a Legislator. That Laws are best ex-
> plained, interpreted, and applied by those whose Interest and Abilities
> lie in perverting, confounding, and eluding them. I observe among you
> some Lines of an Institution, which in its Original might have been tol-
> erable; but these half erased, and the rest wholly blurred and blotted
> by Corruptions. It doth not appear from all you have said, how any
> one Perfection[3] is required towards the Procurement of any one Station
> among you; much less that Men are ennobled on Account of their Vir-
> tue, that Priests are advanced for their Piety or Learning, Soldiers for
> their Conduct or Valour, Judges for their Integrity, Senators for the
> Love of their Country, or Counsellors for their Wisdom. (II, vi, 18)

Part of the humor and the shame of the exposé of Gulliver's England is

---

[2] Orrery, p. 159. cf. Aristotle, *Politics,* III, iv.
[3] A variant reads *Virtue* for *Perfection;* see PW, XI, 307.

that the King condemns on the same basis of justice to which Gulliver appealed. Just as in Lilliput, the most damning standards are those to which the ordinary citizen pays lip service.

Gulliver's phrase for the simplicity of the King (and the laws of his land) is "narrow Principles and short Views." Like the Houyhnhnms, the Brobdingnagians are simple-Lifers: the King, hating all refinement and secrecy,[4] "confined the Knowledge of governing within very narrow Bounds; to common Sense and Reason, to Justice and Lenity, to the Speedy Determination of Civil and criminal Causes" (II, vii, 5). The King's opinion is very close to one expressed by Swift in a letter to Pope: politicians have a maxim which they "themselves do not believe at the same time they practise by it, that there is something profound in politics, which men of plain honest sense cannot arrive to" (C, III, 117).

The Brobdingnagians achieve simplicity (without which Swift believed nothing could be perfect) in their laws by limiting the number of words per law to twenty-two, and by making it a capital crime for any one to write a commentary on any law. Their King, like Thomas Jefferson, is an agrarian philanthropist:

> And, he gave it for his Opinion; that whoever could make two Ears of Corn, or two Blades of Grass to grow upon a Spot of Ground where only one grew before; would deserve better of Mankind, and do more essential Service to his Country, than the whole Race of Politicians put together. (II, vii, 5)

That Swift should so strongly direct the reader's approval of the King's opinion needs accounting for. Swift's interest in gardening and husbandry is clear in his correspondence (C, III, 252, 264, 378; IV, 30, 219, 313). In this attitude he seems to follow Sir William Temple, a horticultural enthusiast of some reknown.[5] Swift's age, moreover, witnessed a vogue of agricultural experimentation and invention. In 1701 Jethro Tull invented the seed drill, and throughout his lifetime argued, to the astonishment of many farmers, the advisibility of hoeing crops regularly to increase the yield.[6] John Laurence, an Anglican rector, published a book in 1726, the title page of which suggests still another source of Swift's agarian sympathies. The three epigraphs on Laurence's

---

[4] See E. B. Benjamin, "The King of Brobdingnag and *Secrets of State*," *JHI*, XVIII (October, 1957), 572–579.

[5] See his essay *Upon the Garden of Epicurus*.

[6] See R. E. Prothero, *English Farming Past and Present* (London: Longmans, Green, 1912), Chapter VII; G. E. Fussell, The *Old English Farming Books from Fitzherbert to Tull* (London: Crosby Lockwood, 1947), Chapter VI, and *More Old English Farming Books from Tull to the Board of Agriculture* (London: Crosby Lockwood, 1950), Chapter I.

title page are from Cicero's *Offices,* Cicero's *Cato major,* and Xenophon's *Economy.*[7]

Many civilizations, of course, have valued agriculture highly. The
ancients, particularly the Romans, seem to have placed an emphasis on
the virtue of farming somewhat similar to the pronouncement of the
Brobdingnagian King. Xenophon, in *Economy,* has Socrates say that
farming "appeared to be held in highest estimation by our states, because it seems to turn out the best citizens and most loyal to the com-
munity."[8] Cato the Censor's views are similar: ". . . when [our fore-
fathers] were trying to praise a good man they called him a good farmer
and a good tiller of the soil."[9] Cicero, like most Romans, including
Virgil in the *Georgics,* pays homage to the agrarian life:

> For my part, at least, I am inclined to think that no life can be happier
> than that of a farmer, not merely from the standpoint of duty performed,
> which benefits the entire human race, but also because of its charm . . .
> and the plenty and abundance it gives of everything that tends to the
> nurture of man and even to the worship of the gods.[10]

The shortness of the King's views and the narrowness of his principles
stem from his and his people's limiting their learning to what Swift
thought the proper objects of knowledge:

> This Prince [Gulliver relates] took a Pleasure in conversing with me;
> enquiring into the Manners, Religion, Laws, Government, and Learn-
> ing of Europe. . . . His Apprehension was so clear and his Judgment
> so exact, that he made very wise Reflexions and Observations upon all
> I said. (II, iii, 9)

Gulliver had earlier noted that the King "had been educated in the
Study of Philosophy, and particularly Mathematicks" (II, ii, 5), but
later he discovers how limited this study was:

> The Learning of this People is very defective; consisting only in Moral-
> ity, History, Poetry and Mathematicks; wherein they must be allowed
> to excel. But, the last of these is wholly applied to what may be useful in

---

[7] John Laurence, *A New System of Agriculture: Being a Complete Body of
Husbandry and Gardening* (London: Tho. Woodward, 1726).

[8] Xenophon, *Economy,* tr. E. C. Marchant (London: Heinemann, 1923), VI,
7–10.

[9] *Cato the Censor on Farming.* tr. Ernest Brehaut (New York: Columbia University Press, 1933), p. 1. Pliny the Elder quotes him thus: "The agricultural class
produces the bravest men, the most gallant soldiers and the citizens least given to
evil designs," *Natural History,* tr. H. Rackham (London: Heinemann, 1950),
XVIII, vi, 26.

[10] Cicero, *De Senectute,* tr. W. A. Falconer (London: Heinemann, 1923), XVI,
56.

Life; to the Improvement of Agriculture and all mechanical Arts; so that among us it would be little esteemed. And as to Ideas, Entities, Abstractions and Transcendentals, I could never drive the least Conception into their Heads. (II, vii, 6)

In addition to his advocacy of justice and simplicity, the King is a humanitarian. The ethical contrast between Gulliver and the King is thrown into high relief when Gulliver offers him the secret of gunpowder.[11] This high point of ethical conflict is at the same time Gulliver's most ambitious moment: a diminutive insect in Brobdingnag, he yet hopes to do the King a great favor. The episode ends with Gulliver's most bitter humiliation and with the triumph of the King's humanitarianism. Gulliver lamely slaves his pride by deriding the King's lack of interest in enslaving his people, merely "from a nice unnecessary Scruple, whereof in Europe we can have no Conception" (II, vii, 5). Of course, since the invention of airplanes and hydrogen bombs, Europe is in a fairer way of having some conception of such a scruple. "A Voyage to Brobdingnag" can be understood as an anti-Machiavellian satire. Swift's prince, unlike Machiavelli's, is not *ostensibly* "merciful, faithful, humane, sincere,"[12] he is truly so, and extremely critical of pretense to these virtues in Gulliver and his civilization. The clearest instance of the King's anti-Machiavellianism is his refusal of the offer of gunpowder.[13] As did Gulliver, Machiavelli offered the princes of his day "explosive" information: how to succeed in politics. Considering Machiavelli's writing in the worst light, we can assume that he could not imagine a prince refusing such information which would make controlling one's subjects so easy. In the episode in which Gulliver offers the secret to the King, Swift hit upon a brilliant way to illustrate the inhumanity and injustice, if not of Machiavelli's teaching, at least of Machiavellianism.

The King's refusal of a modern invention suggests further a larger

[11] That Swift lets Gulliver make this offer may have some connection with the ancient-modern quarrel in which Swift and Temple had once been engaged. Temple, who Ehrenpreis feels was a model for the King of Brobdingnag (*The Personality of Jonathan Swift* [London: Methuen, 1958], pp. 92 ff.), granted the Moderns superiority in two inventions, the loadstone and gunpowder. His judgment on the two, however, has often been overlooked: ". . . both these have not served for any common or necessary Use to Mankind; one having been employed for their Destruction, not their Preservation; and the other, only to feed their Avarice, or increase their Luxury," "Some Thoughts upon Reviewing the Essay of Antient and Modern Learning," *The Works of Sir William Temple* (London, 1720), I, 303.
[12] See Chapter XVIII of *The Prince*. Swift seems to follow Thomas More; R. W. Chambers interprets Utopia as "a protest against the New Statesmanship: against the new idea of an autocratic prince to whom everything is allowed," *Thomas More* (Ann Arbor: University of Michigan Press, 1958), p. 131.
[13] He is also of the kind of magnanimity represented by Gulliver in Part I.

object of satire: modernism, Swift's old enemy.[14] The King's champion-
ing of the traditional understanding of justice and his abridgment of
learning to the humanities (the arts and useful sciences) oppose him to
the rise of modern political theory, of modern science, and of modern
education. In this voyage Gulliver (representing modern man) stig-
matizes himself as proud, cruel, unjust. On the positive side of the satire
is the grand figure of the King—just, humane, sensible, clear-sighted.
And also severe—as Gulliver remarks, "And I would be hard indeed, if
so remote a Prince's Notions of Virtue and Vice were to be offered as a
Standard for all Mankind" (II, vii, 2). The King is the most striking
presentation of Swift's ideal of the truly heroic.

[14] Cf. Leo Strauss's comment on "the possibility that Swift was right when he
compared the modern world to Lilliput and the ancient world to Brobdingnag,"
"Preface to the American Edition," *The Political Philosophy of Hobbes* (Chicago:
University of Chicago Press, 1963), p. xv.

CHAPTER 8

"Of Darkness from Vain Philosophy, and Fabulous Traditions"

Just as the voyage to Lilliput is a record of the good-natured Gulliver's initiation into the complexities of human viciousness, the voyage to Laputa is an account of the quite sensible Gulliver's experience with a number of errors of the mind, or follies. The title which Hobbes gave to Chapter XLVI of *Leviathan* summarizes Swift's purposes in Part III: "Of Darkness from Vain Philosophy, and Fabulous Traditions." In the episodes of the flying island, the progressivism of Balnibarbi, and the scientific projectors of the Academy of Lagado, Swift satirizes the follies of natural philosophers and scientific projectors, and the imprudence of those who rush from the tried and tested to the newfangled. Gulliver's visits to the school of political projectors, to the island of sorcerers, and to the court of Luggnagg form something of a treatise on injustice and an attack on certain "fabulous traditions" in political history and political philosophy. Gulliver's last adventure, except for his experiences with the Japanese and the Dutch in his efforts to return home, concerns a "common Imbecility of human Nature," the belief that immortality is blissful or that long life is a good in itself.

I

THE IMPROPER USE OF HUMAN REASON

In this voyage Swift turns to a favorite theme, as in his most scintillating satire, *A Tale of a Tub*: "Abuses and Corruptions in Learning" (PW, I, 6). A now sane and rational Gulliver first confronts the citizens of the Flying Island—which is an imaginative creation of a human Cloud-Cuckoo-Land.[1] But, of course, the satire on the abstracted life of the intellect in Swift's Flying Island is closer in spirit to the satire of yet another of Aristophanes' plays, *The Clouds*. The Laputans lost in

---

[1] Cf. Aristophanes' *The Birds*. See *The Peace, the Birds, the Frogs*, tr. B. B. Rogers (London: Heinemann, 1930), p. 213.

thought on their flying rock resemble Aristophanes' Socrates, deep in contemplation in a think-basket tied high among the rafters. Both satirists ridicule abstracted intellects for their neglect of the common and necessary forms of life. A lizard causes the caricature of a gaping Socrates to lose a grand thought;[2] flappers are needed to keep the Laputans from "falling down every Precipice" (III, ii, 1). The Laputans' devotion to the inner life of the intellect leads them to follow theory to the detriment of practice, the folly of which is impressed on Gulliver with clarity when an abstracted tailor makes him a suit of clothes by first measuring him with quadrant and compass (III, ii, 7).

> Their Houses are very ill built, the Walls bevil, without one right Angle in any Apartment; and this Defect ariseth from the Contempt they bear for practical Geometry; which they despise as vulgar and mechanick, those Instructions they give being too refined for the Intellectuals of their Workmen; which occasions perpetual Mistakes. . . . I have not seen a more clumsy, awkward, and unhandy People. (III, ii, 11)

They cannot understand any subjects but their favorites; they reason badly, are argumentative, and have no "Imagination, Fancy, and Invention" (III, ii, 11). Gulliver, like his creator, finds them "disagreeable Companions" (III, iv, 2).

Swift's satire is a spiritual descendant of Aristophanes' in still another respect. In *The Clouds* Aristophanes is clearly decrying the loss of the tried, the tested, the traditional—which loss he attributed to the new intellectual influences of Socrates and the Sophists.[3] Swift makes the same point in his projection of the choatic "modernism" or "progressivism" of Balnibarbi, the land over which the Laputans rule. Swift leaves little doubt that his Sophists are modern scientists: "About Forty Years"[4] before Gulliver's visit:

> . . . certain Persons went up to Laputa, either upon Business or Diversion; and after five Months Continuance, came back with a very little Smattering in Mathematicks, but full of Volatile Spirits acquired in that Airy Region.[5] . . . these Persons upon their Return, began to dislike the

---

[2] Aristophanes, *The Clouds*. See *The Acharnians, the Knights, the Clouds, the Wasps*, tr. B. B. Rogers (London: Heinemann, 1927), p. 279.

[3] *Ibid.*, p. 391.

[4] Marjorie Nicholson and Nora Mohler ("The Scientific Background of Swift's *Voyage to Laputa*," *Annals of Science*, II [1937], 318) subtract 40 from 1726, the date of the publication of *Gulliver*. It better suits their argument, and makes more sense, to subtract the number of years Gulliver specifies from the date at that point of the voyage: 1707–1708. Forty years back would be in the 1660's—about the time of the founding of the Royal Society, which was chartered in 1662, 1663, and 1669.

[5] Obviously this connection between the speculative folly of pure science and the applied nonsense of experimentalists is somewhat allegorical. It may be interpreted as Swift's opinion of the causal connection in fact between the two activities in history.

Management of every Thing below; and fell into Schemes of putting all Arts, Sciences, Languages, and Mechanicks upon a new Foot. To this End they procured *a Royal Patent* for erecting an Academy of Projectors[6] in Lagado: And the Humour prevailed so strongly among the People, that there is not a Town of any Consequence in the Kingdom without such an Academy. (III, iv, 14; italics mine)

These projectors "contrive new Rules and Methods" for every human undertaking and wreak havoc in industry and agriculture. Illustrating perfectly Swift's technique of satire by means of contrast is the old-fashioned gentleman, Lord Munodi, who has the only prosperous lands and attractive houses to be seen in Balnibarbi. Frowned on by his neighbors as a "well-meaning Man, but of low contemptible Understanding," Munodi is a conservative traditionalist; his house, for example, a noble structure, was "built according to the best Rules of ancient Architecture" (III, iv, 9, 12).

Besides the obvious imprudence of the projectors in abandoning proven methods for wild schemes, Gulliver implies that they are at fault in several more particulars. He has some of the humanists' contempt for the perverse and indecent (ungentlemanly) interests of the "scientists." In the Grand Academy "the most ancient Student" still works to discover "an Operation to reduce human Excrement to its original Food" (III, v, 3–4); and there is a "great Physician" who inflates a dog with a pair of bellows. While Gulliver is visiting the latter experimentalist the dog dies, and Gulliver leaves as the physician tries "to recover [the dog] by the same Operation" (III, v, 11). These scientists, so it seemed to Gulliver, are trying to achieve things impossible to be done. They brazenly meddle with nature, even trying to improve on it,[7] and others of their fellows are doing the same. One has "been Eight Years upon a Project for extracting Sun-Beams out of Cucumbers, which were to be put into Vials hermetically sealed, and let out to warm the Air in raw inclement Summers" (III, v, 3). Another tries to "sow Land with Chaff, wherein he affirmed the true seminal Virtue to be contained" (III, v, 13). And a third hopes to be able "to prevent the Growth of Wool upon two young Lambs; and he hoped in a reasonable Time to propagate the Breed of naked Sheep all over the Kingdom" (III, v, 13). There is much wit in the skillful touch, "in a *reasonable* Time," for the word reasonable is violently out of place, in the midst of such insanity.

[6] This substantiates the argument of note 4.

[7] For a poetic discussion by a scientist of modern man's inclination to "improve on nature once he gets the idea," see Loren Eiseley, "The Bird and the Machine," *The Immense Journey* (New York: Random House, 1955).

This remarkable undertaking, Gulliver feels, along with the Laputan engrossment in mathematics and music, springs "from a very common Infirmity of human Nature, inclining us to be more curious and conceited in Matters where we have least Concern, and for which we are least adapted either by Study or Nature" (III, ii, 12). Modern science, in Swift's time, was exulting in the certainty resulting from its new experimental and mathematical bases and complacently condemning the errors of the ancients, especially Aristotle. When Gulliver visits the island of the sorcerers he calls up first Aristotle and then the moderns, Descartes and Gassendi:

> . . . with whom I prevailed to explain their Systems to Aristotle. This great Philosopher[8] freely acknowledged his own Mistakes in Natural Philosophy, because he proceeded in many things *upon Conjecture as all Men must do*; and he found, that Gassendi, who had made the Doctrines of Epicurus as palatable as he could, and the Vortices of Descartes, were equally exploded. He predicted the same Fate to Attraction, whereof the present Learned are such zealous Asserters. He said, that new Systems of Nature were but new Fashions, which would vary in every Age; and even those who pretend to demonstrate them from Mathematical Principles, would flourish but a short Period of Time, and be out of Vogue when that was determined. (III, viii, 2; italics mine)

I am not sure that the twentieth century can quarrel with the proposition that yesterday's astronomy is today's astrology. Swift seems to have felt that the inner causes and aspects of nature are simply not to be known; and it might be added, should Swift's case need support, that he and Berkeley are in agreement in this matter.[9]

The reader does not have to turn back to the Second Voyage to discover the proper objects of human knowledge. Gulliver complains that the Laputan king "discovered not the least Curiosity to enquire into the Laws, Government, History, Religion, or Manners of the Countries where I had been" (III, ii, 18), whereas Gulliver is pleased that "a great Lord" of the court, the only man there "adorned with Integrity and Honour" showed a great interest in exactly those things which his king ignored—that is, roughly, the humanities (III, iv, 4).

Finally, the learning of Laputa and Lagado stands condemned, in Gulliver's mind, of having a base motivation. The Laputans betray the fact that their learning is a vanity or affectation in forming a "very mean Opinion" of Gulliver's intelligence when he refused the offices of a flapper; they eagerly converse with him in order to raise his "Admiration of their great Abilities" (III, ii, 3–4). Like a true scientist, a professor

[8] See note 40, Chapter 4.
[9] See George Berkeley, *The Principles of Human Knowledge*, Part I, Nos. 1–10.

in the academy is seeking to reduce the discovery of truth to a method
—by means of his invention, a great frame which contained all the
words in the language on revolving blocks:

> Every one knew how laborious the usual Method is of attaining to Arts
> and Sciences; whereas by his Contrivance, the most ignorant Person
> *at a reasonable Charge, and with a little bodily Labour,* may write Books
> in Philosophy, Poetry, Politicks, Law, Mathematicks and Theology,
> without the least Assistance from Genius or Study. (III, v, 15; italics
> mine) [10]

The professor is careful to ask that Gulliver, on his return to England,
"do him Justice, as the sole Inventer of this wonderful Machine" (III,
v, 18). The same easy learning is sought by a mathematician in the
Academy, who hopes to develop a wafer which teaches whoever swal-
lows it the proposition and demonstration written on it (III, v, 24).

II

A "Treatise" on Injustice and Tyranny

Although the scientific projectors Gulliver encounters seem to prove,
to his satisfaction, that some uses to which reason is put are imprudent,
indecent, futile, and often motivated by vanity, ambition, and laziness,
the "School of political Projectors" does not seem to be a den of fools at
all. Rather it seems to have a function in a different kind of satire, not
directed so much against false learning as against injustice in politics,
especially in modern politics and modern political theory. This is clear
from the beginning of the episode, where Gulliver, for the first time in
the voyage, speaks foolishly, or probably ironically; in any event, Swift's
purpose is clear:

> In the School of political Projectors I was but ill entertained; the Pro-
> fessors appearing in my Judgment wholly out of their Senses; which is
> a Scene that never fails to make me melancholy. These unhappy People
> were proposing Schemes for persuading Monarchs to chuse Favourites
> upon the Score of their Wisdom, Capacity and Virtue; of teaching Min-
> isters to consult the publick Good; of rewarding Merit, great Abilities,
> and eminent Services; of instructing Princes to know their true Interest,
> by placing it on the same Foundation with that of their People: Of
> chusing for Employments Persons qualified to exercise them; with many

[10] The words which I italicize point up a similarity to positivistic methods in the
social sciences, where with a little money and labor one can set up controlled experi-
ments to prove that people tend to think of famous cities as larger than less famous
ones, or that most people think a certain way is "up," another "down." Gulliver
describes such an experiment perfectly as a "Project for improving speculative
Knowledge by practical and mechanical Operations" (III, v, 15).

other wild impossible Chimaeras, that never entered before into the
Heart of Man to conceive; and confirmed in me the old Observation,
that there is nothing so extravagant and irrational which some Philosophers have not maintained for Truth. (III, vi, 1)

The flexibility of Swift's satiric technique is especially clear here, for the
professors do not represent folly, but rather are devices for satirizing
political vices, especially injustices. This section on injustice and tyranny
properly begins with a definition of justice (couched in the irony of the
passage just quoted) as ruling for the common good and dispensing
honors and offices to the virtuous and talented.[11]

However, not all the projectors are so visionary. One doctor

... had very usefully employed his Studies in finding out effectual Reme-
dies for all Diseases and Corruptions, to which the several Kinds of
publick Administration are subject by the Vices or Infirmities of those
who govern, as well as by the Licentiousness of those who are to obey.
(III, vi, 2)

This looks like a squib at Hobbes' expense, since he worried more about
the obedience of the subject and the vigor of administration than about
the injustice with which the administrator may act.[12] This impression is
reinforced by the following sentence: ". . . all Writers and Reasoners
have agreed, that there is a strict universal Resemblance between the
natural and the political Body" (III, vi, 2). It was Hobbes who in
Swift's day was remembered for this comparison, which was made at
the very beginning of *Leviathan*. Gulliver's projector refines on this
notion so that physic will be given to members of a senate to restore them
to healthful legislation, just as one would administer medicine to a sick
person (III, vi, 2).

The various other political "projects" reflect, among other things, on
the "short and weak Memories" of ministers, on senators who invariably
vote against the public interest, on the mentality of those who engage
in party politics. Of these perhaps one deserves some explication: a professor has written something like a white paper on excremental tests for
plots to overthrow the government. Gulliver contributes a suggestion
that a ministry, if it suits its advantage, can find a plot in any innocent
papers, if it deciphers the words cleverly or makes out acrostics. This

---

[11] See Chapters 2 and 3.
[12] See *Leviathan*, XXI (139): ". . . nothing the sovereign can do to a subject, on
what pretence soever, can properly be called injustice or injury." An early critic of
Hobbes' philosophy argued that there is a law above tyranny, a law by which kings
are bound—Roger Coke, *Justice Vindicated from the False Fucus* [sic] *Put upon It
by Thomas White Gent., Mr. Thomas Hobbes, and Hugo Grotius* (London: G.
Bedell, 1660), pp. 31–33.

bitterly humorous satire on the injustice and cruelty of political revenge, derives from the experience of Swift's friends (Oxford, Bolingbroke, Ormonde, and Atterbury) at the hands of the Whig secret committee, which tried to find and invent incriminating evidence (III, vi, 4–15).

Gulliver's voyage to Glubbdubdrib, the Island of Sorcerers, although a separate episode, continues the satire on injustice, principally the injustice of tyrants. Since the spirits of the dead, whom the sorcerers can conjure up, can tell no lies, Swift can facetiously use this ancient satirical technique to dispute a few supposed facts in recorded history. But historians do not bear the blunt of the satire:

> I desired that the Senate of Rome might appear before me in one large Chamber, and a modern Representative, in Counterview, in another. The first seemed to be an Assembly of Heroes and Demy-Gods; the other a Knot of Pedlars, Pick-Pockets, Highwaymen and Bullies. (III, vii, 9)

Caesar and Brutus are made to appear:

> I was struck with a profound Veneration at the Sight of Brutus; and could easily discover the most consummate Virtue, the greatest Intrepidity, and Firmness of Mind, the truest Love of his Country, and general Benevolence for Mankind in every Lineament of his Countenance. I observed with much Pleasure, that these two Persons were in good Intelligence with each other; and Caesar freely confessed to me, that the greatest Actions of his own Life were not equal by many Degrees to the Glory of taking it away. I had the Honour to have much Conversation with Brutus; and was told that his Ancestor Junius, Socrates, Epaminondas, Cato the Younger, Sir Thomas More and himself, were perpetually together: A Sextumvirate to which all the Ages of the World cannot add a Seventh. (III, vii, 10) [13]

By the luckiest chance in the world, Gulliver's opinion is here identical with Swift's; and if there ever was a sextumvirate which Swift aspired

---

[13] Swift's reverence for Roman virtue is discussed in Chapter 4. Such an attitude was hardly a rarity in the Renaissance and the Enlightenment. Unqualified praise was given Cato, for example, by Addison in his play, by François M. C. Deschamps in his *Cato*, tr. John Ozell (London: J. Morphew, 1716), and by Theobald Lewis in *The Life and Character of Marcus Cato*, 2nd ed. (London, 1713). The sceptical humanist to whom Swift is often compared, Montaigne, had written that Cato "was verily a pattern that Nature chose to show to what height human virtue and constancy can reach." Montaigne also had spoken very clearly about his reverence for ancient virtue: "Crawling in the slime of the earth, I do not fail to exalt to the clouds the inimitable greatness of some heroic souls." See *The Essays of Montaigne*, tr. E. J. Trechmann (London: Oxford University Press, 1927), I, 229, 228. It is conventional to speak of Montaigne's early stoical period, the principles of which he himself repudiates in "Apology for Raymond Sebond." But his very last essays (e.g., "Of Experience") show an enduring admiration for the classics, for the wise men and heroes of classical antiquity. Cf. Donald M. Frame, "Introduction," *The Complete Works of Montaigne* (Stanford: Stanford University Press, 1957), p. xii.

to swell to a septumvirate, it was this one. The virtue which Gulliver
describes Brutus as possessing is exactly that to which Swift was all his
life a votary.[14]

Gulliver's tyrannophobia[15] is as fierce as Swift's and his love of liberty
and classical antiquity is as warm:

> It would be tedious to trouble the Reader with relating what vast Num-
> bers of illustrious Persons were called up, to gratify that insatiable De-
> sire I had to see the World in every Period of Antiquity placed before
> me. I chiefly fed mine Eyes with beholding the Destroyers of Tyrants
> and Usurpers, and the Restorers of Liberty to oppressed and injured
> Nations. But it is impossible to express the Satisfaction I received in my
> own Mind, after such a Manner as to make it a suitable Entertainment
> to the Reader. (III, vii, 11)

Characteristically, after such a climax, Swift's satire skips playfully
around, touching on assorted subjects, but notably on two ancients
whom Swift admired, Homer and Aristotle, before returning to the
denigration not only of tyrants but of royalty and nobility generally. By
calling up the dead, Gulliver discovers that the lineages of kings and
noblemen in modern times are anything but pure and uninterrupted
(III, viii, 4). There follows a paragraph which is usually called a satire
on writers of history; it is just barely that, for most of the satire concerns
bigger fish. Swift is soon off on his favorite themes, the scarcity of virtue
and the prevalence of injustice:

> I was chiefly disgusted with modern History. For having strictly ex-
> amined all the Persons of greatest Name in the Courts of Princes for an
> Hundred Years past, I found how the World had been misled by prosti-
> tute Writers, to ascribe the greatest Exploits in War to Cowards, the
> wisest Counsel to Fools, Sincerity to Flatterers, Roman Virtue to Be-
> trayers of their Country, Piety to Atheists, Chastity to Sodomites, Truth
> to Informers. How many innocent and excellent Persons had been con-
> demned to Death or Banishment, by the practising of great Ministers
> upon the Corruption of Judges, and the Malice of Factions. How many
> Villains had been exalted to the highest Places of Trust, Power, Dignity,
> and Profit: How great a Share in the Motions and Events of Courts,
> Councils, and Senates might be challenged by Bawds, Whores, Pimps,
> Parasites, and Buffoons: *How low an opinion I had of human Wisdom
> and Integrity*, when I was truly informed of the Springs and Motives
> of great Enterprizes and Revolutions in the World, and of the contempt-
> ible Accidents to which they owed their Success. (III, viii, 5; italics
> mine)

[14] See Chapter 4.
[15] The term is Hobbes' in *Leviathan,* **XXIX** (214). Significantly, the satire on
tyranny and the praise of resistance to tyrants in Part III begin in Gulliver's first
adventure among the Laputans. See III, iii, 10–14.

From three kings he learns what a stranger justice is at courts:

> . . . they did never once prefer any Person of Merit, unless by Mistake
> or Treachery of some Minister in whom they confided: Neither would
> they do it if they were to live again; and they shewed with great Strength
> of Reason, that the Royal Throne could not be supported without Cor-
> ruption; because, that positive, confident, restive Temper, which Virtue
> infused into Man, was a perpetual Clog to publick Business. (III, viii,
> 6)

By the standards of justice introduced ironically at the beginning of
Chapter VI, the kings stand damned for their injustice; and perhaps we
get a clue as to Swift's motive in Gulliver's apology: "I hope I may be
pardoned if these Discoveries inclined me a little to abate of that profound Veneration which I am naturally apt to pay to Persons of high
Rank, who ought to be treated with the utmost Respect due to their
sublime Dignity, by us their Inferiors" (III, viii, 7). Gulliver's experience in Glubbdubdrib is an education in the sham and injustice of
modern notions of absolutism and divine right of kings, when judged by
the standards of justice and classical republicanism.

Investigating further into the true history of the past, Gulliver discovers that virtue is never, or seldom, regarded; a consideration of a
case of virtue ignored, in fact punished, in Rome of Augustus' day leads
Gulliver to inveigh against the "Force of Luxury" in corrupting Rome
so quickly, just as the pox and luxury have resulted in the degeneration
of the English:

> I descended so low as to desire that some English Yeomen of the old
> Stamp, might be summoned to appear; once so famous for the Sim-
> plicity of their Manners, Dyet and Dress; for Justice in their Dealings;
> for their true Spirit of Liberty; for their Valour and Love of their Coun-
> try. Neither could I be wholly unmoved after comparing the Living
> with the Dead, when I considered how all these pure native Virtues were
> prostituted for a Piece of Money by their Grand-children; who in selling
> their Votes, and managing at Elections have acquired every Vice and
> Corruption that can possibly be learned in a Court. (III, viii, 12)

Whatever the accuracy of Gulliver's picture of the Roman virtue of the
English yeomen before 1660, there can be no doubt that such is the
virtue Swift wanted to find in all men.

Swift's satires often drop to a lower key at the point of greatest intensity of meaning and moral fervor. After the spirited assault on the corruptions of modern kings, noblemen, and commoners Gulliver gives a
calm account of his visit to the King of Luggnagg. Gulliver sends to the
court a request that he may

> . . . have the Honour to lick the Dust before [the King's] Footstool. This is the Court Style, and I found it to be more than a Matter of Form: For upon my Admittance two Days after my Arrival, I was commanded to crawl upon my Belly, and lick the Floor as I advanced. (III, ix, 4)

Out of deference to Gulliver, a stranger, the floor had been cleaned; but often it was "strewed with Dust on purpose" for enemies of the court. "Neither is there any Remedy, because it is capital for those who receive an Audience to spit or wipe their Mouths in his Majesty's Presence." This formality, however, has some utility:

> When the King hath a Mind to put any of his Nobles to Death in a gentle indulgent Manner; he commands to have the floor strowed with a certain brown Powder, of a deadly Composition, which being licked up infallibly kills him in twenty-four Hours. But in Justice to this Prince's great Clemency, and the Care he hath of his Subjects Lives, (wherein it were much to be wished that the Monarchs of Europe would imitate him) it must be mentioned for his Honour, that strict Orders are given to have the infected Parts of the Floor well washed after every such Execution; which if his Domesticks neglect, they are in Danger of incurring his Royal Displeasure. I my self heard him give Directions that one of his Pages should be whipt, whose Turn it was to give Notice about washing the Floor after an Execution, but maliciously had omitted it; by which Neglect a young Lord of great Hopes coming to an Audience, was unfortunately poisoned, although the King at that Time had no Design against his Life. But this good Prince was so gracious, as to forgive the Page his Whipping, upon Promise that he would do so no more, without special Orders. (III, ix, 4)

Will any one suggest that this satire is negative?—that concepts of justice and humanity do not here by implication in the irony point up the willful inhumanity and injustice of kings? This kind and just king encourages Gulliver to stay at his court, but Gulliver, with good reason, finds it not "consistent with Prudence and Justice" to do so (III, ix, 7).

III

A "COMMON IMBECILITY"

While in Luggnagg, Gulliver hears about the Struldbrugs, the exceptional Luggnaggians who live forever, before having seen one of them. Gulliver goes into benevolent raptures at the thought of so blessed a group; at the prompting of one who knows them well, Gulliver imagines what he would do if he were a Struldbrug. He would amass a store of wealth; he would then get all knowledge and wisdom; he would then teach the young "of the Usefulness of Virtue in publick and private Life"; he would help support his fellow immortals, stand as a bulwark against the corruption of time and the natural course of "Degeneracy of human Nature," and witness the great historical and natural evolutions and the progress of the sciences (III, x, 7–8).

The company that Gulliver is in is well entertained by his sanguine betrayal of a "common Imbecility of human Nature." In Luggnagg the presence of the immortals—who at ninety lose their health, their sense, their memories, and their natural affections—is a corrective for that imbecility. In Luggnagg "the Appetite for living was not so eager," contrary to the pattern of behavior in the rest of the world, where one rarely hears "of any Man who died willingly" (III, x, 11–12). The effect of the Struldbrugs on Gulliver, predictable enough, yet takes an odd republican turn: he remarks that his "keen Appetite for Perpetuity of Life was much abated. I . . . thought *no Tyrant* could invent a Death into which I would not run with Pleasure from such a Life" (III, x, 21; italics mine).

IV
The Structure and Coherence of "A Voyage to Laputa"

Book III contains eleven chapters: the first and eleventh, according to the pattern of all four books, concern the events leading up to Gulliver's landing in the hitherto unknown lands and the manner of his return to England. Also, the first and last chapters treat a common theme: the mercy and lenity of the pagan Japanese in contrast with the hypocrisy and cruelty of the Christian Dutch (cruelty and humanity form a theme throughout Book III). In the last chapter Gulliver gets permission to refrain from the ritual usually imposed on the Dutch by the Japanese, "trampling upon the Crucifix." But a Dutch captain turns informer, telling the authorities, who have imperial orders to let Gulliver refrain, that Gulliver has not yet trampled on the cross: for which he is soundly beaten by the Japanese officer in charge (III, xi, 4–5). The pagan has more Christian virtue than the "Christian"![16]

Four chapters (II–V) concern the follies of scientists and projectors; four chapters (VI–IX) deal with injustice and tyranny (or with certain false political doctrines); and one chapter (X) is an account of Gulliver's losing a fear of death. The coherence of the voyage and the interconnection of its themes should be clear: Swift's main interest in scientists and projectors concerns their moral and political influences—how much folly do they introduce into public affairs? In the episodes of Chapters VI to XI the satire continues to be directed against political

---

[16] This odd notion recurs in a little poem; see C, III, 293.

evils, but of greater consequence. The heroes whom Gulliver encounters
are the enemies of tyrants and the lovers of freedom and justice: for the
good of their countries, or to achieve some great human good, they were
willing to die. Thus the Struldbrug episode has relevancy to Swift's
tyrannophobia: as any active virtue, the virtue to resist injustice requires that one have no fear of death, or at least prefer death to a
certain kind of life. The frame chapters, I and XI, involve the same
cruelty and inhumanity satirized in the chapters on tyrants.

By means of a striking but possibly only fortuitous parallel, the coherence of Book III can be easily indicated. Swift is in partial agreement and remarkable disagreement with Hobbes, and (as noted above)
Book III bears no slight resemblance to Chapter XLVI of *Leviathan,*
entitled "Of the Darkness of Vain Philosophy." The main arguments of
that chapter are briefly as follows: (1) Philosophy, whether mathematical, astronomical, or otherwise, must be useful to human life: true
philosophy is "knowledge acquired by reasoning . . . to the end to be
able to produce, as far as matter, and human force permit, such effects,
as human life requireth." (2) The disputations of the Greek philosophers, or of others who "prate and loiter," are "unprofitable"—"What
has been the utility of these schools?" (3) Aristotle's metaphysics and
physics, which dominate European universities, are replete with "absurdities." (4) The "moral, and civil philosophy" of the ancients "hath
the same, or greater absurdities." The chief of Aristotle's errors is in
distinguishing types of governments, on the basis (Hobbes says) of his
own "appetite" or irrational prejudice: that is, to turn to Aristotle, in
Chapters IV and V of Book III in *Politics*, governments are divided into
two types, the just and the unjust, depending on whether the rulers aim
at their own advantage or the public good: thus monarchy is the just
rule of one man for public good, tyranny the unjust rule of one for
private advantage. This doctrine is anathema to Hobbes, who holds that
the ruler, whether one or many, cannot act unjustly. Hobbes believes
that Aristotle has taught men "to call all manner of commonwealths
but the popular [the democratic] . . . tyranny." This erroneous teaching,
according to Hobbes, has caused "tyrannophobia" and bloody civil
wars.[17]

---

[17] *Leviathan,* XXI (139); See *Leviathan,* XXIX (214), XLIV (448). Edward
Hyde, Earl of Clarendon, disagreed with Hobbes' judgment on the effect of ancient
political science: ". . . whatever errors may have bin brought into Philosophy by
the autority of *Aristotle,* no man ever grew a Rebel by reading him." See *A Brief
View and Survey of the Dangerous and Pernicious Errors to Church and State in
Mr. Hobbes's Book, Entitled Leviathan* (London, 1676), p. 84.

Also, Hobbes argues in Chapter XLVI that "there is another error of Aristotle's politics, that in a well-ordered commonwealth, not men should govern, but the laws."[18] Hobbes' objection to this view should be noted: "What man, that has his natural senses, though he can neither write nor read, does not find himself governed by them he fears, and believes can kill or hurt him when he obeyeth not? Or that believes the law can hurt him; that is, words and paper, without the hands and swords of men?" Then Hobbes shows why such "errors" as Aristotle's are "pernicious": they stimulate the public spirit, love of liberty, and hatred of injustice and tyranny, which Swift admired; ". . . they induce men," Hobbes observes, "as oft as they like not their governors, to adhere to those that call them tyrants [that is, adhere to men like Brutus, who call men like Caesar tyrants], and to think it lawful to raise war against them." (5) There are certain fabulous traditions, such as the legends of saints and miracles "alleged by the doctors of the Roman Church"; these are "errors" and "old wives' fables."

Swift agrees with Hobbes that (1) all knowledge, scientific or not, must contribute to man's well-being, and (2) that merely unprofitable intellectual activities, like those of Laputa, are foolish wastes of time. Yet (3) Swift apparently thinks that physics and metaphysics are matter of "conjecture," outside the bounds of knowledge. And (4) Swift loved the classics for the very reasons that Hobbes hated them. He opposed the almost totalitarian doctrines of obedience to rulers who can do no wrong—Book III is a representation of the injustice of tyrants and their lack of any claim to rulership; Swift is certain that there are laws of justice over the authority of tyrants and that by these laws tyrants do not deserve to rule. Also, the education of Gulliver by the examples of the Struldbrugs tends to contravene one of Hobbes' basic notions. The ultimate passion in man is not fear of death. If a man is cured of his fear of death, as Gulliver was, he can be rational in fearing most of all injustice, a violation of law. It is law, not force, which some men respect most. In the spirit of natural law, as understood by the ancients, Swift disagreed with the authoritarian "power-politics" theories of Hobbes. In fact (5), Swift's corrections in modern history concern the errors or

[18] Aristotle's view, however, needs to be quoted: ". . . it is preferable for the law to rule rather than any one of the citizens, and according to the same principle, even if it be better for certain men to govern, they be appointed as guardians of the laws and in subordination. . . . He therefore that recommends that the law shall govern seems to recommend that God and reason alone shall govern, but he that would have man govern adds a wild animal also; for appetite is like a wild animal, and also passion warps the rule even of the best men. Therefore the law is wisdom without desire" (*Politics*, III, xi, 3–5).

"fabulous Traditions" of historians who, before or after Hobbes, follow his political principles in their histories, which glorify kings no matter how vicious, which tend to induce obedience to and respect for kings, and which unjustly praise the vicious and dispraise the good.

An anti-Hobbist tract in the eighteenth century was an act of piety and justice. "A Voyage to Laputa" is Swift's anti-Hobbist tract.

CHAPTER 9

A Satyr Where He Most Commends

The nineteenth century generally could not bear the Yahoos; the twentieth century cannot bear the Houyhnhnms. The nineteenth century preferred to overlook the sordid and unpleasant; our own century prefers to ignore, or smile at anything edifying, "moral," or "noble." We have said good-bye to all that.

Since the sensibility of our age is allergic to the Houyhnhnms, critics tend to either disapprove of Swift's inventing the repulsive horses,[1] or assume that Swift himself found them repulsive and intended to satirize them.[2] The latter interpretation recommends itself especially because it falls in neatly with a modern critical dogma, that one should never identify the creator-author with one of his creature-characters.[3] This dogma may be reasonable; to be sure that the Houyhnhnms represent Swift's opinions, we need to know (a) what the Houyhnhnms represent and (b) what Swift's opinions are. It is circular, of course, to prove one by the other; both must be known and then compared.

If the reasoning behind the dogma which critics apply to *Gulliver's Travels* is sound, one must take care not to rush out of one fallacy into another. If the Houyhnhnms cannot be assumed to represent what Swift believed, neither can they be assumed to be the opposite of his beliefs. This is the fallacy we need concern ourselves with today, since our not liking the Houyhnhnms is no proof that Swift did not like them. It is probably a strong presumption that he did. Because of the anti-utopianism of our time,[4] only an effort toward detachment will allow us to ask the right questions about the Houyhnhnms: What traits did

---

[1] E.g., George Orwell, *Shooting an Elephant* (New York: Harcourt, Brace, 1950), p. 71.

[2] Kathleen Williams, *Jonathan Swift and the Age of Compromise* (Lawrence: University of Kansas Press, 1958), p. 199.

[3] This is, however, a rule which modern artists themselves do not follow; see Orwell, *Shooting an Elephant*, p. 71.

[4] See José Ortega y Gasset, *The Modern Theme* (New York: Doubleday, 1961), pp. 144–145. A better known antiutopian statement is the epigraph by Nicolas Berdiaeff in Aldous Huxley's *Brave New World*.

Swift give them? How do these traits jibe with the polarities of the satire
in the rest of the *Travels*? And how do the Houyhnhnms relate to the
general tendencies of Swift's ethical thought?

I
The Virtues of the Houyhnhnms

Like the inhabitants of most ideal commonwealths, the Houyhnhnms
abound in good characteristics. They are clean, neat, orderly; they keep
physically fit through exercise (IV, ii, 2, 5; viii, 14–15). They are kind,
decent, and civil.[5] "Friendship and Benevolence are the two principal
Virtues among the Houyhnhnms." But these virtues take a characteristic form: they are "not confined to particular Objects, but universal to
the whole Race"—that is, since the race is confined to one country, they
are essentially public spirited. "For, a Stranger from the remotest Part,
is equally treated with the nearest Neighbour, and where-ever he goes,
looks upon himself as at home." This friendship is not what we would
call emotional or "natural" in the sense that it is natural for one to love
his own family more than others:

> They have no Fondness for their Colts or Foles; but the Care they take
> in educating them proceedeth entirely from the Dictates of Reason. And,
> I observed my Master to shew the same Affection to his Neighbour's
> Issue that he had for his own. They will have it that Nature teaches
> them to love the whole Species, and it is Reason only that maketh a Dis-
> tinction of Persons, where there is a superior Degree of Virtue. (IV, viii,
> 10).

Their high level of civility and sociability has a pleasant and useful con-
comitant: conversation, which together with contemplation (Gulliver
reports) improves their minds (IV, iii, 3; iv, 7). And in their conversa-
tions with each other:

> . . . nothing passed but what was useful, expressed in the fewest and most
> significant Words . . . where no Person spoke without being pleased him-
> self, and pleasing his Companions: Where there was no Interruption,
> Tediousness, Heat, or Difference of Sentiments. They have a Notion,
> That when People are met together, a short Silence doth much improve
> Conversation: This I found to be true; for during those little Intermis-
> sions of Talk, new Ideas would arise in their Minds, which very much
> enlivened the Discourse. (IV, x, 2)

The Houyhnhnms direct their reason into what they regard as the
proper channels; since they do not read or write, their history is tradi-

---

[5] The first and last Houyhnhnm mentioned in Part IV are characterized as gentle
and kind (IV, i, 5–7; xi, 1).

tional and unproblematic, for very few "Events of any Moment" occur
among such a placid, virtuous people (IV, ix, 5).

> In Poetry they must be allowed to excel all other Mortals; wherein the
> Justness of their Similes, and the Minuteness, as well as Exactness of
> their Descriptions, are indeed inimitable. Their Verses abound very much
> in both of these; and usually contain either some exalted Notions of
> Friendship and Benevolence, or the Praises of those who were Victors in
> Races, and other bodily Exercises. (IV, ix, 7)

The extent of their intellectual interests can be seen in Gulliver's description of the subjects of their discourse:

> [These] are generally on Friendship and Benevolence; on Order and
> Oeconomy; sometimes upon *the visible Operations of Nature,* or ancient
> Traditions; upon the Bounds and Limits of Virtue; upon the unerring
> Rules of Reason; or upon some Determinations, to be taken at the next
> great Assembly; and often upon the various Excellencies of Poetry. (IV,
> x, 2; italics mine)

The phrase italicized implies what is not the object of their learning:
the invisible (and thus unknowable) operations of nature. When Gulliver tells his "Master" of the "several Systems of Natural Philosophy" in
Europe, he is amused:

> . . . that a Creature pretending to Reason, should value itself upon the
> Knowledge of other Peoples Conjectures, and in Things, where that
> Knowledge, if it were certain, could be of no Use. Wherein he agreed
> entirely with the Sentiments of Socrates, as Plato delivers them; which
> I mention as the highest Honour I can do that Prince of Philosophers. I
> have often since reflected what Destruction such a Doctrine would make
> in the Libraries of Europe; and how many Paths to Fame would be then
> shut up in the Learned World. (IV, viii, 9)

Swift might well have got such a view of Socrates from Plato's *Apology,*
where Socrates was forced to correct a misconception some Athenians
held (under the influence of Aristophanes' comedies or Socrates' earlier
behavior), that he was one of those philosophers "who speculated about
the heaven above, and searched into the earth beneath." Socrates makes
a declaration, in the *Apology,* which Swift (or Gulliver) may have had
in mind: "If you ask me what kind of wisdom [I possess], I reply,
wisdom such as may perhaps be attained by men, for to that extent I
am inclined to believe I am wise."[6]

---

[6] The problem in speaking of Socrates as opposing the higher flights of speculative
natural philosophy can be seen in the *Apology* itself: he says, "I do not mean to
speak disparagingly of any one who is a student of natural philosophy" (19). Werner
Jaeger defines the "Socratic Problem" in the following way: "These are the two
extreme views of the question. In one, Socrates is not a philosopher at all, but an
ethical inspiration, a hero of the moral life. In the other, he is the creator of specu-

The life of the Houyhnhnms is remarkably simple: they have a small vocabulary and few wants and passions (IV, iv, 4). Insofar as the appetites are concerned, they are perfectly temperate; they (like Cato)[7] copulate only to have offspring, and the noble ones have only two children in a family, "to prevent the Country from being overburthened with Numbers" (IV, viii, 11). The horses, however, must not be completely temperate by nature because great care is given to the development of stoical eating habits in the young, and temperance is one of the "Lessons equally enjoyned to the young ones of both Sexes" (IV, viii, 14). The horses are devoid of any guile, hypocrisy, or mendacity; they are completely honest. In fact, there is "no Word in their Language to express Lying or Falshood" (IV, iii, 4).

In many ways the Houyhnhnms enjoy blessings and virtues which seem impossible to man. They have no diseases and therefore no need for physicians (IV, ix, 5); Gulliver's "Master" cannot even understand sickness: ". . . that Nature, who worketh all things to Perfection, should suffer any Pains to breed in our Bodies, he thought impossible" (IV, vi, 4). Their existence is perfectly tranquil: they are unacquainted with fear (IV, xii, 6) die without concern, and without grief see their friends and spouses "retire to [their] first Mother" (IV, ix, 9).

They are just by nature; no one aspires higher than he deserves. Gulliver's "Master" makes him:

> . . . observe, that among the Houyhnhnms, the White, the Sorrel, and the Iron-grey, were not so exactly shaped as the Bay, the Dapple-grey, and the Black; nor born with equal Talents of Mind, or a Capacity to improve them; and therefore continued always in the Condition of Servants, without ever aspiring to match out of their own Race, which in that Country would be reckoned monstrous and unnatural. (IV, vi, 15)

It should also be noted that their (and our) belief that women deserve as good an education as men is simply a matter of similar elemental justice:

> And my Master thought it monstrous in us to give the Females a different Kind of Education from the Males, except in some Articles of Domestick Management; whereby, as he truly observed, one Half of our Natives were good for nothing but bringing Children into the World: And to trust the Care of their Children to such useless Animals, he said was yet a greater Instance of Brutality. (IV, viii, 14)

---

lative philosophy, which Plato personifies in him;" *Paideia,* tr. Gilbert Highet, (New York: Oxford University Press, 1943), II, 26; cf. pp. 24–25. Swift inclined to the first view.

[7] See Muriel Jaeger, *Experimental Lives* (London: G. Bell, 1932), p. 20.

All differences in social rank depend on the varying capacities for virtue, not on any artificial or conventional distinctions such as sex or wealth (IV, vi, 15): "They will have it that Nature teaches them to love the whole Species, and it is Reason only that maketh a Distinction of Persons, where there is a superior Degree of Virtue" (IV, viii, 10).[8]

The greatest blessing enjoyed by the Houyhnhnms is their inherent goodness—they "are endowed by Nature with a general Disposition to all Virtues" (IV, viii, 9)—and innocence: Gulliver's "Master" is "wholly at a Loss to know what could be the Use or Necessity of practising . . . Vices" (IV, iv, 7). In this respect the Houyhnhnms have happier natures than human beings. This is further evident in the fact that the Houyhnhnms are devoid of pride:[9]

> But the Houyhnhnms, who live under the Government of Reason, are no more proud of the good Qualities they possess, than I should be for not wanting a Leg or an Arm, which no Man in his Wits would boast of, although he must be miserable without them. (IV, xii, 14)

And Gulliver explicitly points out that in Houyhnhnmland there is no "Pride, Vanity or Affectation" (IV, x, 1). Without the self-assertiveness and restive viciousness of a prideful nature, the Houyhnhnms can be truly unselfish and socialistic: the "Master" cannot understand "what Motives" would cause lawyers to injure their fellow creatures; and he does not understand the motive "for Hire," since money is unknown in his country: "For he went upon a Supposition that all Animals had a Title to their Share in the Productions of the Earth" (IV, vi, 1). In the distribution of food and Yahoos, the Houyhnhnms all share alike: "And where-ever there is any Want (which is but seldom) it is immediately supplied by unanimous Consent and Contribution" (IV, viii, 16). Thus their benevolence and love of country has a purity rather scarce in human beings.

In their behavior the Houyhnhnms imitate another island folk, the inhabitants of More's *Utopia*, who likewise were so happily endowed or educated that "The whole ylande is as it were one familie, or household." But More does not imagine his ideal citizens as given inherently happy dispositions by nature; rather the abundance of goods in Utopia is the great force which defeats pride: ". . . seynge there is abundance of all things . . . certainly in all kyndes of lyvinge creatures either feare of

---

[8] Swift's nonegalitarian principles of justice angered Coleridge (as they do modern readers); see Coleridge's *Miscellaneous Criticism*, ed. T. M. Raysor (Cambridge, Mass.: Harvard University Press, 1936), p. 129.

[9] Contrary to recent opinion: see K. Williams, *Swift and the Age of Compromise*, p. 199.

lack doth cause covetousness and ravyne, or in man only pryde, which counteth it a glorious thinge to passe and excel other in the superfluous and vayne ostentation of things. The whych kynde of vice among the Utopians can have no place."[10]

The Houyhnhnms, however, can be completely rational because they have no bad impulses, no disposition toward vices at all: ". . . Reason alone is sufficient to govern a Rational Creature" (IV, vii, 5)—that is, a creature in whom there are no impulses to contravene reason. Thus reason is not "problematical" with them; it is the so-called right reason which man can follow, if his passions do not intervene. The Houyhnhnms therefore, possessed of right reason, are unanimous in their thinking (IV, xii, 6); a reasonable expression by one of them "strikes you with immediate Conviction; as it must needs do where it is not mingled, obscured, or discoloured by Passion and Interest" (IV, viii, 9).

This uniformity of thought, free of conflict and ambiguity, furnishes the reader with the decisive clue to the reason which controlled Swift's choice of the horse as the perfect animal. The Houyhnhnms are a fusion of two natures: the purely rational nature of man and the docile, temperate, intuitive nature of horses.[11] The nature of horses, to one who takes a *gentlemanly* look at their general behavior, is a happy one: most horses seem to lead tranquil, healthy lives; sex is unproblematic (or problematic only at intervals) and natural. Diseases and vices do not seem to proliferate among them. And, to man, traditionally, the horse has been a noble animal.[12] Thus the choice of the horse-form is apt enough, in view of the neoclassical dictum, "follow nature." Horses

[10] Sir Thomas More, *Utopia*, tr. Raphe Robinson (London: J. M. Dent, 1946), pp. 61–66. Cf. R. W. Chambers: "From some aspects Swift seems to be More come to life again; in *Gulliver* he gives to *Utopia* the honour, rare with him, of direct and repeated imitation, and he repays the debt by depicting Thomas More as the one modern man worthy to rank with the five noblest men of antiquity. Swift has been described as the soul of Rabelais in a dry place; we might think of him as the mind of Sir Thomas More without More's patience or More's faith, wandering through desert places seeking rest and finding none. But in nothing is the likeness more strong than in the passion shown by Swift against the futile wars of Christian nations which, when narrated, arouse the disgust alike of the virtuous Houyhnhnms and of the magnanimous giants of Brobdingnag," *Thomas More* (Ann Arbor: University of Michigan Press, 1958), p. 365.

[11] An old habit of European thought regards animals as superior to men in following nature and in being noncompetitive, docile, and temperate. This habit became fashionable in Swift's time. George Boas has studied this, which he denotes "theriophily," in French writers whom Swift may have read. See *The Happy Beast in French Thought of the Seventeenth Century* (Baltimore: Johns Hopkins University Press, 1933). Like Fontaine, Fénelon, Boileau, and Charron, Swift probably was influenced by Plutarch's *Beasts Are Rational* (or *Gryllus*). See the Loeb *Moralia*, XII, ed. Harold Cherness and W. C. Helmbold (London: Heinemann, 1957).

[12] See G. Wilson Knight, *The Burning Oracle* (London: Oxford University Press, 1939), p. 121.

follow nature completely; and the putative etymology of the word *Houyhnhnm* is *"the Perfection of Nature"* (IV, iii, 5).[13] This would seem a tautology, since the Houyhnhnm "Master" thinks it impossible for nature to function imperfectly, as in allowing diseases to exist. Perhaps Swift was profoundly charmed by an idea of great endurance in Western thought, that man can achieve moral and physical health if he follows nature. We can even see the idea often today, for example in a book by a medical doctor, who says, ". . . it seems reasonable to suspect that pathogenic bacteria which are harmful to the body are in the world for another purpose than to cause sickness in human beings."[14]

For satiric contrast, a perfect and authoritative voice for right reason was needed, reason uncorrupted by passion. A perfectly temperate creature is needed to embody right reason; the right reason potential in man is given to an animal with a nature that will allow reason exclusive control. Thus right reason unopposed by a recalcitrant natural disposition results in a characterization of perfect wisdom: Gulliver's impression soon after seeing his first two Houyhnhnms is ironically correct: ". . . if the Inhabitants of this Country [are] endued with a proportionable Degree of Reason, they must needs be the wisest People upon Earth" (IV, i, 6).

The traits[15] which Swift gave the Houyhnhnms are clearly ideal, utopian. That some modern readers cannot accept them, even conditionally, as utopian remains a perplexity. Who, even today, will quarrel with more than three or four of these virtues and traits? Of course the twentieth century will not have any "learning" limited (although it tolerates thousands of men who limit their learning more than the Houyhnhnms do), nor will it allow the notion "right reason" more than a condescending smile. Unanimity, which Swift and Pope thought inevitable and desirable among the good and wise, and even desirable if imposed on a given society,[16] this the twentieth century regards as anathema, but only because we tend to identify it with the worst politi-

---

[13] I am uncertain why this notion of perfection, and others like it usually called Stoic, should be regarded as anti-Christian. See the Sermon on the Mount: "Be ye therefore perfect, even as your Father which is in heaven is perfect" (Matt. 5:48).

[14] D. C. Jarvis, *Folk Medicine* (New York: Fawcett, 1961), Appendix E.

[15] Cleanliness, neatness, industry, love of exercise, kindness, benevolence, pacifism, love of wit and conversation, properly limited learning, intelligence, belief in coeducation, simplicity, temperance, honesty, fearlessness, stoicism, justice, lack of pride, and rationality.

[16] See Pope's letter to Swift, C, V, 31; and Swift's to Pope, C, III, 277. "This devotion to Reason is one of the many striking likenesses between Thomas More and Jonathan Swift. To both of them it appears a tragedy that Reason does not lead men at once to the same conclusions. When Gulliver visited the virtuous horses, he found things different," R. W. Chambers, *Thomas More,* p. 253.

cal movements in modernity: fascism and communism. Indeed, in Western Civilization for a good many years there was something, which (compared to the chaos of modern opinion) looks very like unanimity. Assuredly, the Houyhnhnm notion of justice has little appeal in these days of democratic theory and liberalism—although every profession worth anything at all has heavily institutionalized machinery for honoring the meritorious and paying tribute to merit and virtue.

Even today the traits of the Houyhnhnms are virtues. Or are there those among us who would like to be set down as opposed to cleanliness, neatness, industry, exercise, civility without ceremony, kindness, bravery...?

Modern distaste for the Houyhnhnms is further complicated in that many readers reject the Houyhnhnms but accept the idealism of the other parts of *Gulliver's Travels*. But the idealism throughout the *Travels* is strictly consistent. In Part I how Houyhnhnmlike is the innocent, benevolent Gulliver and the utopian laws of Lilliput—which include stoical education of children and equal education of women! In his views on justice and public spirit, in his opinion about the proper objects of knowledge, in his simple, noble nature, and in his benevolence the King of Brobdingnag conforms to the ideals of Part IV. The King is almost a kind of disproof that the virtues of the Houyhnhnms are such as only rational horses could enjoy; he is proof that the virtues of the Houyhnhnms are not impossibly ideal. The logical necessity of this relationship cannot be ignored: if Swift contemned the Houyhnhnms, so also did he contemn the King of Brobdingnag.[17] Only *after* his experience in the land of horses does Gulliver change his opinion of the King: ". . . the least corrupted," Gulliver at last realizes, "are the Brobdingnagians, whose wise Maxims in Morality and Government, it would be our Happiness to observe" (IV, xii, 4). Part IV, finally, furnishes the positives for the negatives of Part III: cruelty, improper use of human reason, injustice, and inordinate love of living.

Likewise consistent with the virtues of the Houyhnhnms are the

---

[17] The relevance of the second and fourth voyages is suggested in the fact that Gulliver sets out in both in a ship named the *Adventurer*. The ingenuity which has discovered the Houyhnhnms to be an object of satire has not been directed against the King of Brobdingnag. Why is not the latter also the butt of a Christian joke, since he represents a hopelessly grand idea, towering above the human being Gulliver? This grandeur is forever beyond Gulliver's reach, suffering as he does from original sin (symbolized in his comparatively diminutive stature). As Gulliver points out," . . . how vain an Attempt it is for a Man to endeavour doing himself Honour among those who are out of all Degree of Equality or Comparison with him" (II, v, 15). Nonetheless, Gulliver, corrupted by the giants, refuses on his return to England to accept original sin (the smallness of the inhabitants) and foolishly thinks that people ought to be large (i.e., good).

virtues which Swift praised throughout his writings—discussed in Chapters 2, 3, and 4. From his inordinate concern with cleanliness to his despairing appeals to reason (including, too, such pet notions as the education of women, the value of conversation, the worth of exercise[18]), the things he valued most are almost completely identical with the traits of the Houyhnhnms. Yet modern readers find the Houyhnhnms unattractive and cold;[19] they would probably react the same way to Swift's character, if they understood it properly. Like the Houyhnhnms, Swift was sternly high-principled and benevolent; he was not sentimental or warm and openhearted in his good works: as he wrote Pope, "I am utterly void of what the world calls natural affection [that is, sentimental attachment to one's kin], and with good reason, for they [his relatives] are a numerous race degenerating from their ancestors [who are virtuous]" (C, VI, 126).

The same sober, sensible, aloof virtue is found in his heroes, Cato and Brutus. The modern intellectual finds them about as unattractive as the Houyhnhnms.[20] The Houyhnhnms are citizens blessed by Nature with Roman virtue. If all the citizens possess the virtue of Cato and Brutus there is no need for government and, incidentally, no need for the superhuman, heroic virtue which sacrifices itself in standing out against wickedness, or against tyranny, for example. The Houyhnhnms have the temperate, just, benevolent nature of Swift's heroes, but the possibility of great virtuous action is happily denied them, since they have no imposing evils confronting them.

Like Socrates, Cato, Brutus, Sir Thomas More, and Robert of Gloucester, the Houyhnhnms pass the limits of human nature. Some human beings can surpass their peculiarly human limitations; and when they do they approach (Swift believed) the perfection of the Houyhnhnms. Such human beings are rare: seldom are good nature and wisdom combined in the same person.

---

[18] See J, I, 56; II, 401.

[19] Those who teach *Gulliver's Travels* are well acquainted with this response from students, who point out the indifference of the horses when near relatives die (a widow cheerfully visits the day of her husband's death, IV, ix, 8), yet ignore the kindness with which the dying Houyhnhnms are treated by their neighbors: "Some Weeks before their Death they feel a gradual Decay, but without Pain. During this time they are much visited by their Friends, because they cannot go abroad with their usual Ease and Satisfaction" (IV, ix, 9). The words that Joseph Addison lets Cato speak on the death of his son have the same stoic quality as this gentle, calm acceptance of death. Cato asks whether his son died bravely. Told that he did, Cato replied: "I'm satisfy'd." See *Cato* (London: J. Tonson, 1713), p. 52. Perhaps Swift's characterization of the Houyhnhnms owes something to a conviction similar to one of Sir William Temple's, that "Coolness of Temper and Blood, and consequently of Desires, [is] the great Principle of all Virtue." See *Works* (London, 1720), I, 308.

[20] See, e.g., Orwell's remarks, *Shooting an Elephant,* pp. 55–76.

Swift took notice of only two species of beings who act virtuously without hope of reward after death: the ancients and the Houyhnhnms. Swift did not in any way condemn the ancients: how could he criticize them for not being Christian? Rather his admiration was almost unbounded. He thought, however, that for most men, belief in a God and the sanctions of heaven and hell are needed, in the interest of virtue. Swift quarreled with Deists and freethinkers, not because they also admired the ancients, but because they were (he thought) inimicably opposed to traditional Christianity, which they were destroying. Nowhere does he quarrel with what they might have cared to believe privately; in fact, his sermon "On the Testimony of Conscience" is basically deistic and sets forth points I, III, and V of the basic five deistic tenets: [21]

    I. *There is one supreme God.*
   II. He ought to be worshipped.
 III. *Virtue and piety are the chief part of divine worship.*
 IV. We ought to be sorry for our sins and repent of them.
   V. *Divine goodness dispenses rewards and punishments both in this life and the next.*

The last point, for Swift, is the crucial one: "The most considerable among the Heathens did generally believe Rewards and Punishments in a Life to come; which is *the great Principle* for Conscience to work upon" (PW, IX, 156; italics mine). The argument of the sermon further illustrates the deistic coloring of Swift's thought: ". . . a Religious Conscience is the only true solid Foundation upon which Virtue can be built." Few Deists, from Herbert of Cherbury to Benjamin Franklin, would disagree with that proposition.

A bias akin to Deism in Swift's thought need disturb no one who devoutly believes in Swift's "orthodox piety"; historically, the Christian church has accepted the tenets of natural religion (the same as those of Deism), which man had been able to deduce by his reason, before he had the gift of revelation. As E. C. Mossner with succinctness notes, "In addition to this independent Natural Religion, the Christian held the Revelation of the Scriptures. Anyone who accepted the former but not the latter was, in the language of the day, a Deist." [22]

---

[21] As expounded by Lord Herbert of Cherbury in several of his works; see, e.g., *De Religione Laici,* tr. H. R. Hutcheson (New Haven: Yale University Press, 1944), p. 101. Dryden rehearses the same five beliefs as being those of a Deist in *Religio Laici,* 11.42 ff. See E. C. Mossner, *Bishop Butler and the Age of Reason* (New York: Macmillan, 1936), pp. 47 ff.
[22] Mossner, *Bishop Butler and the Age of Reason,* p. 27.

But Swift did oppose Deism (which at that time purposely set out to undermine the authority of revealed religions) as a force which would weaken the established church. He believed that religion needed the authority of both revelation and establishment: the religion necessary to inspire the proper conscience (the proper Deism) must be believed to be the word of God and known to be enjoined and protected by the law of the land.

Now a false argument must be analyzed, a syllogism underlying much of the recent criticism of Part IV:

All Deists are the objects of Swift's satire (dislike).
The Houyhnhnms are (resemble) Deists.
Therefore, they are the objects of Swift's satire (dislike).[23]

But the Houyhnhnms are not even Deists; they are nonbelievers or a-theists (at any rate, Gulliver is silent about their belief or unbelief). They are presented in the last voyage not as embodiments of both man's lights—reason and religion. They represent only the former, rational morality, not both. Reason, Swift believed, is an inadequate guide only because of the frailties of human nature, not because reason does not exist.

Besides, the Houyhnhnms can much more convincingly be shown to embody Swift's dearest principles, than be made to have a superficial resemblance to the Deists. An incidental coincidence has created a rash of critical distortions. Impatient to find a clergyman working within strictly ethical bounds, critics have denied Swift's own ethical beliefs in proving that Part IV is a "defense of Augustinian Christianity."[24] It is best to leave such critics with two questions: to what Deist did Swift ever ascribe even half the excellences of the Houyhnhnms? And, as Thomas Sheridan asked two hundred years ago, ". . . shall they give [Swift] no credit for the exalted view in which he has placed the nobler part of our nature, when wholly under the direction of right reason?"[25]

II

THE SATIRIC PURPOSE OF THE HOUYHNHNMS

Whatever Swift's—or the modern reader's—attitude toward the Houyhnhnms, the function of the horses in the satire of Part IV admits

[23] See the review by R. S. Crane of several articles in *PQ*, XL (July, 1961), 427–430.
[24] Calhoun Winton, "Conversion on the Road to Houyhnhnmland," *Sewanee Review*, LXVIII (Winter, 1960), 21.
[25] Sheridan, p. 435. Sheridan, incidentally, was a Christian, too.

of no misinterpretation. The structure of the satire centers on Gulliver's changing opinion of human nature. The two instruments of change are the Yahoos and the Houyhnhnms.

As soon as Gulliver lands he discovers an animal, the Yahoo, which he immediately detests. His attitude toward human beings is, however, honorific: ". . . There were few greater Lovers of Mankind, *at that time,* than myself" (IV, ii, 5; italics mine). Without any hesitation or qualification, he observes to his Houyhnhnm "Master" that men are "the only governing, rational Animals" in his home country (IV, iii, 14). The action of the first three chapters is so arranged that Gulliver, with his high opinion of mankind, comes first to see the physical resemblance between himself and the "detestable" Yahoos and then to try to prevent the Houyhnhnms from identifying him as a genuine Yahoo. In Chapter II, Gulliver is placed side-by-side one of the "Beasts": whereupon, "My Horror and Astonishment are not to be described, when I observed, in this abominable Animal, a perfect human Figure" (IV, ii, 4). In Chapter III, the Houyhnhnm "Master" discovers that Gulliver has a false covering of clothes, which Gulliver has kept secret "in order to distinguish myself as much as possible, from that cursed Race of Yahoos" (IV, iii, 8), who, of course, wear none. At the end of Chapter III, however, Gulliver still regards men as rational animals and the Yahoos as a "degenerate and brutal" species of man (IV, iii, 14).

In the next three chapters Gulliver tries to give the "Master" an account of human society, or of "what human Nature in our Parts of the World is capable to perform" (IV, iv, 7). This account, under the influence of the horses, turns out to be a diatribe against the standing evils in European civilization: war (its causes and destructiveness), the law and lawyers, money, luxury, wine, doctors and diseases,[26] chief ministers and their lacqueys, and hereditary nobility. Gulliver rightly feels that he needs to give some excuse for his objective and high-minded attack on his own society:

> The Reader may be disposed to wonder how I could prevail on my self to give so free a Representation of my own Species, among a Race of Mortals who were already too apt to conceive the vilest Opinion of Human Kind, from the entire Congruity betwixt me and their Yahoos. But I must freely confess, that the many Virtues of those excellent Quadrupeds placed in opositive View to human Corruptions, had so far opened mine Eyes, and enlarged my Understanding, that I began to view the Actions and Passions of Man in a very different Light. (IV, vii, 1)

[26] On Swift's attitude toward doctors, see J, II, 401.

Thus an attack of a different kind is directed against human nature: first, the physical similarity between Yahoo and man denigrates the human form; now, the virtues of the Houyhnhnms reveal the imperfections of human beings in the truest light. Finally, in Chapter VII, the identity of the moral natures of man and Yahoo is demonstrated by the Houyhnhnm "Master," who considers nearly the same evils which Gulliver found in Europe, as they evidence themselves among the Yahoos: war (the Yahoos, he observes, "hate one another more than they did any different Species of Animals"), money, legal squabbles (with greater theoretical insight, the "Master" considers money before legal matters), diseases and medicine, governors and their toadies, sexual license, filthiness, hypochondria, and female licentiousness and "Scandal." Gulliver begins to speak of man and the Yahoo as one: like the "Master," he believes both are "Animals to whose Share . . . some small Pittance of Reason had fallen, whereof we made no other Use than by its Assistance to aggravate our natural Corruptions, and to acquire new ones which Nature had not given us" (IV, vii, 1–21).

The crisis of Part IV is either the point of Gulliver's recognizing the moral identity of Yahoo and man (Chapter VII), or the point which marks the recurrence and climax of an earlier theme of the book, when a female Yahoo sexually assaults the naked Gulliver: "For now I could no longer deny, that I was a real Yahoo, in every Limb and Feature, since the Females had a natural Propensity to me" (IV, viii, 6–7).

After narrating this episode Gulliver sketches the excellences of the Houyhnhnms in some detail (Chapter VIII–IX). In speaking of their legislative assemblies, Gulliver incidentally tells of "their old Debate," of which he occasions a resumption: "The Question to be debated was, Whether the Yahoos should be exterminated from the Face of the Earth" (IV, ix, 1–2). This betrays in a way the purpose of Part IV: in it the human species is on trial. Gulliver acts as the judge (with the Houyhnhnms) and as the accused (with the rest of mankind). This is his verdict:

> When I thought of my Family, my Friends, my Countrymen, or human Race in general, I considered them as they really were, Yahoos in Shape and Disposition, perhaps a little more civilized, and qualified with the Gift of Speech; but making no other Use of Reason, than to improve and multiply those Vices, whereof their Brethren in this Country had only the Share that Nature allotted them. When I happened to behold the Reflection of my own Form in a Lake or Fountain, I turned away my Face in Horror and detestation of my self; and could better endure the Sight of a common Yahoo, than of my own Person. (IV, x, 4)

Significantly, the Houyhnhnms succeed where the Brobdingnagians fail—in mortifying Gulliver's pride. At first, he himself tells us, he could not understand the term *Yahoo:* ". . . but I was soon better informed, to my *everlasting Mortification*" (IV, ii, 3; italics mine). As the most cursory comparison of his self-interpretation in Part IV with that of Part II reveals, Gulliver is truly humble in Houyhnhnmland and is in no way proud (that is, proud of his human-being-ness). The Houyhnhnms, Gulliver feels, will cure anyone of such a vice:

> For, who can read of the Virtues I have mentioned in the glorious Houyhnhnms, without being ashamed of his own Vices, when he consider himself as the reasoning, governing Animal of his Country? (IV, vii, 4)

Thus the Houyhnhnms are an ideal construct of clear-sighted virtue, designed for the satiric purpose of pointing up human failings and correcting human pride.[27]

III

A CYNIC'S UTOPIA

The Houyhnhnms, who embody nearly every virtue that Swift "endorsed," are sometimes humorously absurd—for example, in threading needles, riding on sleds. The satiric point is that of the *mythe animal:* a cloven-footed beast's doing intricate work or otherwise behaving like a human being is, sadly enough, more a likelihood than is intelligent, nonbestial behavior by human beings, who are so much more gifted in every way.[28]

Gulliver is the greatest puzzle in Part IV. He is inflexibly honest and humble, thanks to the influence of the Houyhnhnms; but he becomes a fool in his imitation of the horses' gait and intonation. As in Brobdingnag, he imitates that aspect of nobler beings which is least proper to

[27] Cf. Hawkesworth's comment: "Such was Dr. Jonathan Swift, whose writings either stimulate mankind to sustain their dignity as rational and moral beings, by shewing how low they stand in mere animal nature, or fright them from indecency, by holding up its picture before them in its native deformity," pp. 70–71.

[28] Cf. R. W. Chambers: "The underlying thought of *Utopia* always is, *With nothing save Reason to guide them, the Utopians do this; and yet we Christian Englishmen, we Christian Europeans* . . .!

"Just as More scored a point against the wickedness of Christian Europe, by making his philosophers heathen, so Jonathan Swift scored a point against the wickedness of mankind by representing *his* philosophers, the Houyhnhnms, as having the bodies of horses. Yet we do not call Swift inconsistent, because he did not live on a diet of oats, or, like poor Gulliver, fall into the voice and manner of horses in speaking. Swift did not mean that all horses are better than all men. He meant that some men are worse than horses. More did not mean that Heathendom is better than Christianity. He meant that some Christians are worse than heathen," *Thomas More*, p. 128

him: he acts like a giant on his return in Part II, and like a horse in his return in Part IV. At unexpected points throughout the voyages he suddenly becomes the gull.

The crucial mistake of Gulliver's is his unmitigated misanthropy: his rationality is upset by his intense emotional hatred of vices and of the viciousness of human beings in general. He foolishly demands of the whole species an excellence possible to perhaps a few. He thinks man a rational animal at the beginning of the voyage and hates man for not being rational at the end. In his hatred of the general corruption of mankind he seems to undervalue, yet recognizes and describes the worth of the "honest" Portuguese, who capture him and treat him with "great Humanity," and of their captain, Pedro de Mendez, who is not only a "wise Man" but the most benevolent, charitable man in the whole of *Gulliver's Travels* (and there are more than a few benevolent men in it.)[29] It is clear, however, that Gulliver's disorder, an inordinate "Antipathy against human Kind," results from the too great attraction of good things, the virtues. By contrast to perfect creatures human beings become repulsive.

Swift's correspondence is helpful in explaining the puzzling twist at the end of Book IV. He wrote to Pope of his intentions in *Gulliver's Travels:*

> I have got materials together towards a treatise, proving the falsity of that definition *animal rationale,* and to show it would be only *rationis capax.* Upon this great foundation of misanthropy, though not in Timon's manner, the whole building of my Travels is erected. (C, III, 277)

As I argued earlier, the definition of man as *animal rationis capax* implies an aristocratic distinction. In general, men are not, cannot be, rational-moral; some men are and can be—for example, Pedro de Mendez. Consider also Swift's self-interpretation to Pope:

> I have ever hated all nations, professions, and communities, and all my love is toward individuals: for instance, I hate the tribe of lawyers, but I love Counsellor Such-a-one, and Judge Such-a-one: so with physicians —I will not speak of my own trade—soldiers, English, Scotch, French, and the rest. But principally I hate and detest that animal called man, although I heartily love John, Peter, Thomas, and so forth. (C, III, 277)

Men in groups, judged by a relentless moral standard, are never innocent; rationality, morality, is never general. But individuals have a capacity for reason and virtue, and thus may be esteemed and loved by

[29] Gulliver and the Lilliputian who warned him in Part I, the King and Glumdalclitch in Part II; Munodi, Marcus Brutus, Epaminondas, Socrates, Sir Thomas More, Cato, and the Japanese officer in Part III; the Houyhnhnms and Pedro de Mendez in Part IV.

Swift: what else is proved by the de Mendez episode? Gulliver himself appreciated de Mendez' virtues; for we judge him by Gulliver's account, which is laudatory.

Gulliver's Travels, Part IV, is then a Cynic's utopia. Diogenes himself wrote a utopia, *The Republic,* which is unfortunately not extant.[30] But the main lines of what a Cynic's utopia would be are clear—without Diogenes' work, and even without *Gulliver's Travels.* The Cynic would project society's own best beliefs (ideals) and inclinations into the uniform principles of utopia. But, in describing what ought to be, the Cynic will bitterly describe it as what is not. In that sense, Cynicism is negative; it emphasizes what good things do *not* exist. Further, the utopian Cynic grows cynical at his own utopianism, at his caring too much about what cannot be, in general.[31] Gulliver is finally the Cynic-gull of Part IV. He grows so chagrined at his species' general behavior that he can hardly accommodate himself to a rare case of human merit, Captain de Mendez. And, alas, a bit of cynicism is even in the name *Mendez,* suggesting as it does "untrustworthiness"—as if the creation of de Mendez is a lie.

It is a mistake to assume that Swift never laughs at himself, the satirist and misanthrope. From his correspondence we know he often felt ignoble in his bitterly emotional reaction to folly and vice, especially among the Irish. If this state of mind has any connection with Part IV then the "fable" of that book perfectly illustrates Swift's mind: that of the unbending Cynical moralist relentlessly putting mankind on trial and condemning it as a species, while being a philanthropist in his private capacity and a patriot in his public capacity. Swift knows and values highly the friendship of a number of men and women like de Mendez and the sorrel nag: Arbuthnot, Gay, Pope, Sheridan, Stella, Vanessa, and many more. His virtue made him hate vices and try to shame men out of them (mortify them). In doing this he often seems as foolish as if he were trying to teach men virtues only to be found in rational horses. But the joke is not only on him; it is on mankind, too.

---

[30] D. R. Dudley, *A History of Cynicism* (London: Methuen, 1937), p. 26.

[31] Although Cynics, historically, never tired of condemning man's general behavior, they were sanguine about their own achievements in virtue; see Dudley, *A History of Cynicism,* pp. ix–x. A famous sentence from Swift's letters shows his awareness of this Cynical attitude, which he pretends to view from a higher vantage: "I tell you after all, that I do not hate mankind: it is *vous autres* who hate them, because you would have them reasonable animals, and are angry for being disappointed" (C, III, 293). Whether Swift was not usually among *les autres* is a basic question facing those who interpret Swift's life and writings. Who—Swift or Pope—bitterly denounced the madness of religious enthusiasts? Who was angry with the Irish? And whose heart was lacerated in largely futile struggles for human liberty?

CHAPTER 10

The Precepts of His Book

In many comments on human nature Swift appears as bleakly cynical as Hobbes, La Rochefoucauld, and Mandeville. And his religious and political philosophy seems based on utilitarian assumptions concerning human motivation. But there is that in his writings which distinguishes him clearly from Hobbism and utilitarianism—namely, a few convictions which place him in an older tradition of ethical philosophy. The force of these convictions can be summarized in seven lines, the burden of Swift's ethics: He believed in simplicity in all things—art, morals, social life, religion. He was convinced of the reality of common sense (rationality, reason), as a thing all-too-seldom met with. He was a champion of humanistic learning, although little known as such. He was the perpetual enemy of cruelty, in the name of kindness. His understanding of justice was classically strict: rule of the virtuous for the common good. Like the Roman republicans, he hated all forms of tyranny. And he persisted, throughout his life, in a worshipful admiration of certain men, who were for him the great models of heroic virtue.

Gulliver's Travels, in its own oblique and inimitable way, is Swift's *Prelude,* an account of the poet's mind, a compendium of his ethical thought. Its themes and struggles are the themes and struggles of his entire career.

The structure of "A Voyage to Lilliput" develops out of an opposition of vices and virtues, an opposition real to Swift from his political experience: between cruelty, viciousness, ingratitude and good nature; between injustice and public service; between human pretense and human performance; between original good order and subsequent decay. "A Voyage to Brobdingnag" continues the contrast between petty viciousness and good nature, except that here Gulliver is the negative force. The King becomes the representative of Swift's virtues: justice, public spirit, humanity, and properly directed learning and political wisdom. As an insectlike courtier, Gulliver stands for his civilization at its worst: fiercely destructive, ambitious, irrepressibly proud, unprincipled, "Machiavellian."

In Parts III and IV the technique becomes more subtle and complicated. Gulliver in "A Voyage to Laputa" is the embodiment of good
sense and political wisdom, opposing the madness which he encounters
in the useless abstracted learning of the Laputans and the "progressivism" or "scientism" of Balnibarbi. As an exponent of classical republicanism and justice, Gulliver (in his adventures with the political projectors, with dead kings and heroes called up by the sorcerers, with the
King of Luggnagg, with the Struldbrugs, with the Japanese and the
Dutch) discovers and points up the errors of Hobbist political and
moral doctrines and continues the satiric attack on cruelty and inhumanity and injustice.

Part IV has a different type of title: "A Voyage to *the Country of the*
Houyhnhnms," and it differs in content from the other three. The con-
trasts of the earlier voyages seem dim in comparison to that between
the Houyhnhnms and the Yahoos—the one embodying all the important virtues which Swift praised, the other all the vices he condemned. Like the heroes he admired, Swift's horses exceed the limits of
human nature: with a nature inclined only toward good, they are
perfectly rational and benevolent. The Yahoo, and man in general,
combines an inclination toward vice with reason, which tends to degenerate into a tool for refining and multiplying vices. In Part IV
Gulliver becomes a symbol of the satirist, a man admiring the noble and
good qualities of human beings while hating a little too strongly the base
and evil. Such a Cynic-satirist is not a hater of mankind. Romantic
enthusiasts such as Shelley have confused the idea in the word *love,*
as in love of humanity. To love mankind does not mean to do so as a
mother is supposed (by modern psychologists and social workers, by the
makers of modern novels, modern movies, and modern dramas) to love
her children: a mother must love her children, it is said, follies, vices,
and all. A contrary understanding of philanthropy is that one loves the
best in man (the virtues) and that to love mankind is precisely to wish
the best for it. Swift was aware of man's capacity for goodness (man is
capax rationis) as well as of man's general inclination toward vice. Part
IV is a story of despairing benevolence, the folly of wanting men to be
better than they can be.

Gulliver's (and his creator's) good wishes and despair can be seen in
the letter to Sympson:

> Behold, after above six Months Warning, I cannot learn that my Book
> hath produced one single Effect according to mine Intentions: I desired
> you would let me know by a Letter, when Party and Faction were ex-
> tinguished; Judges learned and upright; Pleaders honest and modest,

with some Tincture of common Sense; and Smithfield blazing with Pyramids of Law-Books; the young Nobility's Education entirely changed; the Physicians banished; the Female Yahoos abounding in Virtue, Honour, Truth and good Sense: Courts and Levees of great Ministers thoroughly weeded and swept; Wit, Merit and Learning rewarded; all Disgracers of the Press in Prose and Verse, condemned to eat nothing but their own Cotten, and quench their Thirst with their own Ink. These, and a Thousand other Reformations, I firmly counted upon by your Encouragment; as indeed they were *plainly deducible* from *the Precepts* delivered in my Book. (PW, XI, 6–7; italics mine)

Yet the positives in *Gulliver's Travels* do not need commentary; they are indeed obtrusive. One can justly complain that there are too many good principles and too many good characters in the *Travels*. Episode after episode implies or directly affirms the goodness of justice, humanity, public spirit, wisdom, the study of the humanities. The protagonists in this satiric narrative are tainted with kindness, integrity, honesty, public spirit, tyrannophobia, and heroism—for example, Gulliver in Part I; the King and Glumdalclitch in Part II; Munodi, Marcus Brutus, Junius Brutus, Epaminondas, Socrates, Sir Thomas More, Cato, and the old English Yeomen of Part III; the Houyhnhnms and Pedro de Mendez in Part IV.

In view of his readers' habit of ignoring all but the negative in his satire, Swift did well to let Gulliver write to Sympson that the *Travels* set forth positive precepts—Swift's principles of virtue, which he explains near the end of the book: ". . . the first Principles of Honour, Justice, Truth, Temperance, publick Spirit, Fortitude, Chastity, Friendship, Benevolence, and Fidelity" (IV, xii, 6).

However incensed he was at the Yahoo in man, and however savage his satire, Swift never disavowed the existence and continued possibility of virtuous and heroic action.

INDEX